# The Ult  Wicca Astrology and Tarot Cards:

*A BOOK UNCOVERING MAGIC MYSTERY AND SPELLS*

**Julia Steyson**

**© 2018**

# THIS BUNDLE INCLUDES THE FOLLOWING BOOKS:

Wicca Spell Book: The Ultimate Wiccan Book On Magic And Witches A Guide To Witchcraft, Wicca And Magic In The New Age With A Divinity Code

## AND

Astrology Uncovered: A Complete Guide to Horoscope and Zodiac Star Signs

## AND

Tarot Cards: A Beginners Guide of Tarot Cards: The Psychic Tarot Manual

# COPYRIGHT

**The Ultimate Guide on Wicca Astrology and Tarot Cards: A Book Uncovering Magic Mistery and Spells**

**By Julia Steyson**

without written consent and can in no way be considered an endorsement from the trademark holder.

# TABLE OF CONTENTS

# WICCA SPELL BOOK:

# CHAPTER 1: THE ORIGINS OF WICCA

Witches. Flying on broomsticks, wearing all black, huddled over cauldrons. Our pop culture idea of witches is full of images like that: green skin, a warted long nose. But as we grow older and wiser, we come to learn that witches are not as we have learned in our childhoods. While these tales may be good for entertainment, there is a rich spiritual history behind Witchcraft that is missed by these caricatures.

It is common and psychologically normal for people to fear what they don't understand. Our society has feared witches for centuries. Hundreds or even thousands of witches were killed in

The Inquisition, witch hunts, and crusades. So much has been lost in the confusion that many people couldn't even begin to tell you what a witch is, or what witches believe and practice.

Today our society copes with the fear of that unknown by making a gentle mockery of a beautiful ancient tradition called Wicca. In this book, geared towards absolute beginners, we will hopefully shed some light on The Old Religion and its adherents.

The goal of this book is not only to educate, but to inspire. Even if you don't leave this book practicing Wicca, the hope is that you will find an understanding with those who do practice, and maybe also find a deeper appreciation for nature along the way.

However, this book serves not only as an educational guide for the curious, but can be used as an instructional how-to-begin for those who *are* interested in beginning their Wiccan journey. Simple explanations about holidays and beliefs are given, and the later chapters directly address how to begin practice, while the early chapters are more for educational purposes.

There are more than a few rich traditions that fall under the umbrella of the term Wicca. In this chapter we will discuss the founding of Wicca, the influences on the religion, how Wicca is distinct from Paganism, and what the Wiccan ties are to magic. This chapter will also take a look at the different traditions of Wicca that have developed over time.

## THE FOUNDING OF WICCA

Wicca is actually a modern religion, with fairly recent roots, though it was not originally referred to as Wicca. The birth of what we know as Wicca traces back to 19th century Britain, which was in the midst of an occult revival movement.

Gerald Brousseau Gardner (1884-1964) is often credited with founding in the 1920s what would expand into Wicca in the 1960s. Gardener studied the anthropological theory by Margaret Murray. This theory posited that an ancient pagan religion had been practiced during the rise and spread of Christianity in Europe. Murray called this religion a "witch cult" and postulated that those who practiced it did so in 13-person covens. Murray also wrote that they worshipped a "horned" god.

In the early 1940s, Gardener's extensive study of Murray's work as well as his deep interest in other authors who specialized in the Occult, inspired him to start his own coven. This was known by its members as the Bricket Wood coven.

In the beginning, around the 1920s-1950s before the term Wicca evolved with the New Age movement, they called it The Craft or The Old Religion. Gardner expanded the religion to include worship of a goddess and the Divine Feminine, along with elements of things he had learned from freemasons and ceremonial magic. We will discuss magic and its place in Wicca more later in the chapter.

Gardner became friends with another early influencer of Wicca in 1947, Aleister Crowley (1875-1947). Crowley was known far and wide for his writings on the occult that were based on his personal experiences participating in a wide range of esoteric religious traditions throughout his life. He travelled around the globe learning about Buddhism, Kabbalah (Jewish Mysticism, astrology, Tarot, and Hindu practices as well.

Crowley is credited with being the first to distinguish magick with a "k" from magic. This was done so that there would be a specific word to differentiate his own religious practices from ceremonial magic, and stage magic that was popular during that time. Gardner adopted many rituals developed by Crowley.

However, nowadays Wiccans prefer to distance their practice from the influential Crowley because of his reputation as a misogynist and a racist. Discriminatory and bigoted perspectives are not considered to be compatible with the Wiccan way of life.

Crowley was also part of the reason Wiccan practices became publicly associated with Satanism. However, this connection is a false one; because Wicca is based on pre-Christian world views and concepts, Satan is not involved in any Wiccan ritual. In fact, Wiccan practice discourages any sort of "black magic" or association with evil.

This tradition is known today as Gardnerian Wicca. It brought many interested women occultists to his coven, including another influential person named Doreen Valiente (1922-1999). She became the High Priestess at Bricket Wood in the early 1950s. Valiente began a long period of religious revision in the material of the coven, in no small part to remove the association the coven had with Aleister Crowley.

Valiente felt that Crowley had made a mistake trying to mass market Witchcraft. Crowley was also known for silencing women who disagreed with them, limiting their participation in his rituals and in the Bricket Coven.

In 1957, Valiente began her own coven. She wrote several books and learned alongside many prominent occultist figures of the New Age religious movement. Valiente emphasized individualism in practice, and is a large reason the practice of Wiccans today is so diverse and varies so much between individuals and covens. Valiente really was the one who took Wicca from being a secretive practice done behind closed doors to w widespread phenomena that many people suddenly had access to because of her work.

In the 1970s Wiccan traditions finally made it out of England thanks to some other key influencers, who brought the Craft to the entire UK, the United States, and Australia. Because of this branching out, many different traditions formed. These traditions include those such as the Dianic, the Celtic, and the Georgian.

Alex Sanders (1926-1988) later founded what is now known as Alexandrian Wicca, which follows a specific set of traditions.Another sect was founded by Raymond Buckland in the 1970s, known as the Seax-Wica tradition. Buckland wrote dozens of books on The Craft and is known as the person who brought Gardnerian Wicca to the United States.

## LATER DEVELOPMENTS

Around the 1980s, Wicca had an estimated 50,000 self-proclaimed Wiccans that in some way practiced in the Northern Americas and western Europe. That growth slowed down significantly by the end of the century, but Wicca gained a considerable amount of social acceptance in that time. Wicca also continued to develop, with new rituals and practices being developed by new Wiccans with every passing generation that upheld the Craft.

The Dianic Wiccans saw Wicca as a woman's religion, and the Neo-Pagan movement began to gain speed alongside Wicca. Neo-Paganism and Wicca are now represented to the world through two international organizations, the Universal Federation of Pagans and the Pagan Federation.

# SHAMANISM

Many Wiccan practices are based in the concept of shamanism. *Shamanism* is an umbrella term for a lot of different practices. It began as an Eastern practice of advanced uses of herbal medicine. Shamans were highly revered in their societies for their medical skills and their ability to communicate directly with the spirit world. A shaman was often identified by having some kind of physical defect, seen as a trade for their special abilities.

Classical shamanism in Northern Asia believed that a shaman was aided by a spirit or even a group of spirits that helped them to heal and to divine the future.Shamans could also connect with guardian spirits, who might be otherworldly or a lifetime partner in the mortal plane.

Shamans channeled the spirit world using sound and music, utilizing tools such as rattles, drums, and improvised songs to conduct their practices.This would most often be done by entering a trance state of consciousness.

Modern Wiccans no longer use the word Shaman, but instead have switched to the term "hedge witch". This will be explained in more detail in Chapter 6. Modern hedge witches channel the spirit world through trance, astral projection, and lucid dreaming.

# PAGANISM AND NEO-PAGANISM

The term *Paganism* has long been used as a derogatory word for all non-Christian (primarily polytheistic) religions. For a long time the word served the same purpose as calling someone a heathen. However, in the modern day, Pagans and Neo-Pagans are reclaiming the title and the faith. While Wicca is considered a Pagan religion and is represented internationally by Pagan Federations, there are distinctions to be drawn between those who identify as Wiccans and those who identify as Neo-Pagans.

Pagan is used today as another umbrella term. According to the Pagan Federation International, "Pagans may be trained in particular traditions or they may follow their own inspiration. Paganism is not dogmatic. Pagans pursue their own vision of the Divine as a direct and personal experience."

One can see that Wicca easily fits within this definition of Pagan. There are traditions that can be chosen and adhered to within Wicca, but this is not a necessity to be a Wiccan (thus it is not a dogmatic religion). Wiccans also have a personal relationship with the Divine and with their individual practices.

So what is a Neo-Pagan, and how are Neo-Pagans different from Wiccans? The answer may depend on who you ask. Because the definition of Pagan is so intentionally vague, it can be hard to draw lines deciding where one tradition begins and where another ends.

According to Joanne Pearson, an occult writer, Wicca is both at the center of and on the margins of Neo-Paganism. The former is stated because the history of Wiccanism and Neo-Paganism has a very large amount of overlap; at the core, they were both born out of the 19th century Occult movement and popularized through the New Age Movement in the 1960s and 1970s.

# MAGIC

In what way is Wicca inherently tied to magic? Some Wiccans would offer that Wicca is in no way inherently related to magic! This is because some Wiccans don't include any magic elements in their practices. That's right -- you can be Wiccan without practicing magic! Many Wiccan rituals are focused around revering nature and don't focus on supernatural elements.

That being said, there are many for whom their Wiccan practices are inseparable from magic practices. There are, as was mentioned much earlier in the chapter, distinctions to be drawn between different types of magic.

*Ceremonial magic*, also known as High Magic, predates almost anything else that Wiccans and Pagans draw from. This kind of magic is known for being elaborate in its ritual. Sometimes this magic is done to appease a God by collecting a variety of different things that would please that deity and using them in a specific manner and order. For this reason, ceremonial magic is also known as ritual magic; the two terms are often used interchangeably.

*Practical magic* is magic that is used in one's day to day life. Sigils, simple spells, enchantments...the purpose of this kind of magic is to make a small, but direct change to everyday life by channeling your own personal magic. This is what is sometimes referred to as magick. This book will use the "k" spelling to distinguish that this is the type of magic being discussed.

# IS WICCA A RELIGION?

This question is a deceptively difficult one to answer. First of all, it depends on how one defines religion. Many definitions of what a 'religion' is have been specifically written to disclude nature-based religions, including Wicca and First Nations religions. Some consider this to be a form of supremacy, while other Wiccans would rather be distanced from organized religion in the first place.

Whether or not Wicca is considered a religion by the world at large, is it considered to be a religion by adherents of Wicca? While some would say yes, I think it's important to consider the voices of Wiccans who would say no. Some Wiccans consider Wicca to be a practice rather than a religion.

This is partially because most organized religions are composed of Orthodoxy and Orthopraxy. Orthodoxy is when one holds "correct" beliefs and is generally considered by Wiccans to be dogmatic and against Wiccan values. Orthopraxy is "correct" practice, which while important to Wiccans, there is no supreme doctrine to determine what the correct way to practice Wicca is.

Some Wiccans that adhere to a specific tradition may value orthopraxy, but no Wiccan would ever tell another Wiccan how to practice authoritatively. Instruction is given through a loving intention, not because there is a right or wrong way to do something.

Some Wiccans don't identify Wicca as a religion because they believe it is a specific decision *against* religion. Others consider it to be a universal religion. Like many things in Wicca, there is no definitive, dogmatic yes or no answer.

# DIFFERING TRADITIONS

As you've seen by now, there are many different traditions that have developed over the course of the history of Wicca. This is undoubtedly because of the influence of Doreen Valiente, who emphasized the importance of individualistic practices and beliefs in her influential books during the rise of early Wicca.

In this subsection we will discuss just a few of the main traditions of Wicca, although many Wiccans consider themselves to practice outside of the guidelines of these traditions. Even a Wiccan living outside a tradition may pull rituals from traditions that speak to them.

*Gardnerian* Wicca focuses on recreating the original teachings and rituals of Gerald Brousseau Gardner himself. Gardner painstakingly recreated rituals he had extensively researched, and wanted to challenge mainstream religion. For example, many of the rituals are performed without any clothes on, to become closer to the natural state. Rituals are focused on nature and involve a creative, bright use of color to represent elements and energies. However, this tradition is also very rule-based, and many have found it to be somewhat constricting.

*Alexandrian* Wicca was founded by Alex Sanders, who was the self-proclaimed "King" of the witches in his coven. Alexandrian Wicca can seem very similar to Gardnerian, mimicking their naked rituals and coven rites, but has more ancient Jewish influences from Kabbalah.

*Georgian* Wicca was founded by George Patterson in California in the 1970s. While Georgian Wiccans follow the general example of Gardnerian Wicca and Alexandrian Wicca, the coven is much more flexible and individualistic. Coven members sometimes make up their own rituals. Patterson used to say regarding rituals, "If it works, use it. If it doesn't, don't."

*Dianic* Wiccan, named after the Greek Goddess Diana, was founded by Zsuzsanna Budapest. Since its inception in 1970s, Dianic Wicca has been known as a particularly feminist branch of the Craft. Only goddess figures are worshipped, and many covens only accept women. Dianic Wiccans are also known for their political activism.

*Eclectic* Wicca is a fast-growing tradition that believes that no formal tradition or doctrine is necessary for one to be a true Wiccan. Eclectic Wiccans ignore institutions that are in place such as initiation, secrecy, and the hierarchical structures of covens.

# CONCLUSION

We've now gotten a taste for the beginnings of what we today know as Wicca. We've discussed history and related terms, and traditions that Wicca has pulled from to become the complete, independent religion (or religion alternative) it is today.

But if one can truly be a Wiccan without subscribing to a tradition, then what exactly is it that makes someone a Wiccan? Well, although beliefs vary widely from Wiccan to Wiccan, there are some core beliefs that most Wiccans hold. These will be discussed in the coming chapter.

# CHAPTER 2: WICCAN BELIEFS AND

# PRACTICES

Modern Wiccans hold a wide range of beliefs and practice is very individualistic, making it hard to define Wiccan beliefs in an exact way. There are, however, some more common, core beliefs that most Wiccans ascribe to. For example, this chapter will discuss that many Wiccans engage with elemental magic, Tarot, and celebrate the festivals of The Wheel of the Year. Esbats and Animism will also be discussed in this chapter to gain a well-rounded grasp on general Wiccan ideals and practices.

The core of Wiccan beliefs teaches us that our practice is our own as long as we are doing no harm to others. Unless you have taken the role of a High Priestess or a Coven Mother, or some other teaching role, it is discouraged to instruct others on how to perform their Craft. Of course offering helpful tips is no problem, but imposing your rules on someone else is against the Wiccan way of life.

All Wiccans, whether they practice magic or not, have a worldview focused on reverence for nature. The Divine lies all around us in the spirits that inhabit us and the natural world. Everything is connected, and a Wiccan treads lightly to maintain the harmonious balance of the Mother Earth.

All Wiccans also worship feminine aspects of the divine alongside their masculine counterparts. In order for there to be balance in the universe, there must be balance among masculine and feminine spirituality and worship.

## THE WHEEL OF THE YEAR: CELEBRATING SABBATS

The Wheel of the Year is the name given to the cycle of festivals held annually by Wiccans and also some Neo-Pagans. Wiccans celebrate all eight festivals of the Wheel of the Year. The solstices and equinoxes make up four of the eight holidays and are known as the quarter days or cross-quarter days. They are the midpoint festivals of the year, celebrating the seasons.

A *solstice* is a celestial event, where the Sun is positioned in its most Northerly or Southerly quadrant in its travel relative to the equator of the Earth. There are two solstice events a year. While the names for festivals vary widely between different Wiccan traditions, the names commonly used for the solstice celebrations are the Midwinter Yule festival and the Midsummer Litha festival.

The *Yule* festival has been celebrated since the late Stone Age. It is known as the turning point of the year, and for many is the most important festival to honor in the entire year. The Sun is an important symbol during this festival, its ebbing in the sky during sunset often seen as a symbol of renewal, fertility, and rebirth.

The Yule festival is celebrated in many various ways, depending on the person, the coven, and the Wiccan tradition being emulated. Common celebrations include making sacrifices, feasting, and giving gifts to those you care about are common elements. Decorations include evergreen plants such as pine and seasonal winter plants such as holly. Tree decorating is also a Wiccan practice at this time, similar to current western Christian traditions for Christmas

The *Litha* festival is one of four solar events being celebrated as well as being a solstice event. This summer festival celebrates the sun shining for the longest of any day of the year. Bede writes that "Litha means *gentle* or *navigable*, because in both these months the calm breezes are gentle and they were wont to sail upon the smooth sea."

The Litha festival is typically celebrated by going outside and reconnecting with nature while the sun is shining. Hikes and drum circles are common celebratory events held. Prayers are said to honor the season, and this is also known as a time of learning and charity within the Wiccan community.

An *equinox* is another celestial event, when the center of the Sun crosses over the equator of the Earth. This occurs twice a year. The equinox festivals are known as the Ostara festival for the Vernal Equinox, and the Mabon festival for the Autumnal equinox.

*Ostara* is the Spring equinox celebration, during which day and night stand exactly equal in time, with light on the increase. Some celebrate on the day of the equinox, while others celebrate Ostara on the full moon after the equinox because of the festival's association with the feminine and the Goddess Aphrodite.

During Ostara Wiccans eat traditional vegetable and herb based dishes, using whatever spring ingredients are native to their area. Floral incense is used, traditionally jasmine or rose. Daffodils and Violets are fresh flowers that are often used in Ostara rituals to promote prosperity in the time of coming light, sometimes in combination with the stone Jasper.

The festival *Mabon* is also known as the Harvest Home, and the Ingathering Feast. Mabon is celebrated in the autumn and is a time to give thanks to th universe, nature, and deities for the annual gifts we have received. Like Ostara, the day is divided equally into night and day, but this time we are paying respects to the coming days of darkness.

Mabon is celebrated by making offerings in thanks for the gifts nature and the Gods and Goddesses have given us. In the Druid tradition, offerings are made to celebrate the fruit-giving trees. Offerings most often include ciders and wines, along with autumn herbs. This celebration is one of the most lavish, and Wiccans often wear their best finery.

The secondary holidays are often cause for large celebrations as well, despite being less important celestial events. These holidays are generally called Imbolc, Beltane, Lammas, and Samhain.

*Imbolc* usually occurs on the first day of February and is a celebration of the first inklings of spring beginning to sprout through the winter frost. Historically a Celtic holiday, for Wiccans this is a time to purify oneself and one's tools, and to do spring cleaning. Dianic Wiccans have coven initiations during this time, and for all Wiccans it is representative of renewal of faith and dedication to the Craft.

Traditionally on the first day of summer in Ireland, *Beltane* also has Celtic roots. Beltane was traditionally to celebrate Flora, the Goddess of flowers. Dancing around a lively bonfire is the most common way Wiccans celebrate this time of season. In duotheistic Wiccan lore, this is the time when the Horned God and the Triple Goddess are perfectly united.

*Lammas* is celebrated on the first day of August and is another Harvest festival. This holy day is to celebrate living off the land, to celebrate grains in particular in the early beginnings of fall. It is common to weave dolls out of grain husks such as corn husks to honor the Gods and Goddesses of the harvest.

Commonly celebrated by non-Wiccans as Halloween, *Samhain* is often a favorite celebration of Wiccans everywhere. Opposite the yearly calendar to Beltane, Samhain is a holiday to honor those who have passed into the great beyond. Ancestors, elders, friends, and even pet familiars are honored at this time. It is a holiday to show love to all those that have passed who have supported us, and those who continue to support us each day.

Samhain is typically celebrated by connecting with the spirit world in some ritual way, because Wiccans believe this is the time of the year that the veil between the natural and the supernatural is the thinnest. Samhain is also spent lighting candle vigils for those we choose to honor and remember on this Day of the Dead.

# ESBATS: HONORING THE MOON

An *Esbat* festival is a festival which is intended to show honor and respect for the moon and Her influence on the natural world. It is a time in which the coven gathers besides the main Wheel of the Year celebrations or the Sabbat. Janet Farrar, a known occultist writer, describes esbats as an opportunity for a "love feast, healing work, psychic training and all."

Esbats occur on a full moon. Some covens that focus on the moon in particular extend these practices to dark moons, and to the first and last quarters of the moons during the month. While the main festivals are times for celebration, the important magickal work of the year is completed during the Esbats.

An Esbat traditionally begins at midnight and finishes at the break of dawn, called cock-crow by many traditional Wiccans for this ritual. Esbats are a complete celebration of the feminine, and the full moon represents Mother Earth impregnated with spiritual energy. Dancing, singing, and magickal rituals are common at Esbats. If one is not part of a coven, often this is done amongst other Wiccan friends.

If the Esbat is done during a full moon, this considered to be one of the most powerful times to perform magick. Crystals and stones are charged with the raw healing and purifying energy of the full moon. Other things, such as water and Tarot decks may be charged with this energy as well, along with a large list of other magick tools.

During a dark moon, however, Wiccans abstain from magick practices. Instead, the focus is turned on inner demons. Meditation and trance states are common ways that dark moons are honored. The goal during a dark moon is to address and conquer the darkness which exists inside all of us.

The waxing of the moon, when the moon is growing larger, is a good time for "positive" spells -- spells that help you gain things like love and wealth. The waning of the moon is a good time for "negative" spells -- spells that help you lose bad habits, or leave something spiritually blocking behind.

The Moons of different months have different names that go along with their different energies. These different energies are important to be aware of, as they may make particular times of year perfect for certain magickal goal.

The January Moon is known as The Wolf Moon or The Winter Moon. Seen as a time to remember things that are coming to an end and also a time to look forward to new beginnings, this moon represents protection and strength.

The February Moon is also known as The Storm Moon or The Death Moon. In centuries past, the brutal cold of this month made it a time of hardship for those practicing the Old Religion who lived off the land. This is a time for spells focused on fertility for the coming Spring.

The March Moon is often called The Chaste Moon or The Seed Moon. This is a time to plant "seeds" in your mind. You press ideas of imagination, creativity, and prosperity, and speak them into existence with chants, spells, and songs. This month of purity and newness is the perfect time to prepare yourself for the coming flora of Spring.

The April Moon is also known as The Egg Moon or The Grass Moon. If you keep a magickal garden, this is the perfect time to begin planting under the Esbat moons. While in March we sowed seeds of the mind, now we sow literal seeds into the Earth. April is a time for action.

The May Moon is sometimes called The Hare Moon or The Flower Moon. This opens the gates of love and romance. This is a good time for love spells and to focus on your romantic partner(s). Rekindling the spark in a relationship is never more possible than during a May Esbat ceremony.

The June Moon is The Lovers Moon or The Rose Moon. This passionate time is perfect for spiritually encouraging romantic engagements and marriages. This is also a time for those who are single to engage in spiritual prosperity spells.

The July Moon, also known as The Mead Moon or The Lightning Moon, is a time of health and enchantment. Mead is the nectar of the Gods, and the time for prosperity and strength is on the rise now powered by the heated energy reflected from the Summer sun.

The August Moon is called The Red Moon. This occurs during Harvest time, a time of abundance. This is another month where marriage magick is strong, and where the fruits of the prosperous summer are given thanks for.

The September Moon is also known as The Harvest Moon. Following August this is another month of abundance during which thanks are given for the fruits of the Autumnal harvests. The Harvest Moon can help bring you and those you care about much prosperity, which you may need in the harsher months to come.

The October Moon is often called The Blood Moon. This is a time of renewal of faith and dedication to the Craft. This is a great time to set new goals for the coming Winter season. Divination is also fueled by extra spiritual energy during October Esbats, so the time for Astrological and Tarot readings is nigh.

The November Moon, sometimes known as The Snow Moon, acknowledges the passing of the abundance of the past seasons. This is a time to connect spiritually with those who mean the most to you, whether they're family, friends, coven members, or your community at large. Emotional bonds can be made stronger through rituals during The Snow Moon Esbats.

The December Moon is also known as The Oak Moon or The Cold Moon. Because the nights have become longest at this time of the year, this is a time to reflect on the true power of the moon. The Moon has dominion over the spirit world during December because the nights are longer than the days. The thoughts of Wiccans turn again towards rebirth and the promise that Spring will return again. Let go of the negative and let the light of the day live on through your spirit during this dark time of year.

# ASTROLOGY

You've probably heard of astrology at one point in your life, and might even know your astrological Sun Sign (sometimes called a Zodiac Sign), because it's based on your birthday - Sagittarius, Capricorn, or what have you.

For centuries people have been using the celestial bodies to predict mundane, worldly events in our lives. Many Wiccans also believe that the stars have a large amount of influence over world events and human emotions. *Astrology* is a type of divination that focuses on interpreting patterns in the planets, Moon, and stars in order to foresee earthly events.

Only since our modern era of scientific revolution took hold did Astrology become discredited as an actual science itself. Thus, it is no surprise that there is much research and nuance behind it that can make astrology seem intimidating and complicated. However, the rich balance between rules and intuition are part of what makes Astrology so effective and attractive to some Wiccans.

Astrology draws on Hellenistic philosophy as well as the model of physics introduced to the world by Aristotle. This means that Astrology regards the movement of the celestial bodies as eternal, while the motions of the four elements (Fire, Earth, Air, and Water) are linear.

Astrology has never been intended to be an exact science, because no one person can truly, completely understand the order of the cosmos. This is also because while Astrology is made to predict trends in human mood and behavior based on the effect of the stars, having divined these things, humans are capable of changing the outcomes despite the influence of the celestial bodies. Divine intervention is another possibility.

Most of us know our Sun Sign, which is the principle sign that forms our personality according to Astrology. There are 12 houses in each person's natal charts, based on where each planet, Moon, or star was when that person was born.

These 12 houses interact with one another to create your full, incredibly nuanced personality. Your Moon Sign, for example, affects the manifestation of your Sun Sign. An emotionally-in-touch Cancer might gain vanity and confidence from having their Moon Sign positioned in Leo, for example. Other planets control other domains in your life. Venus reigns over one's love life, and the Midheaven sign gives us insight into our life's work.

Each astrological sign is related to a planet, an element, and also has a special relationship with either male or female energy. The chart below is a handy way to check out which ones align with your sign!

| Sign | Date | Nature | Element | Planet | Symbol |
|------|------|--------|---------|--------|--------|
| Aries | March 20 – April 20 | Masculine | Fire | Mars | Ram |

| | | | | | |
|---|---|---|---|---|---|
| Taurus | April 20 – May 21 | Feminine | Earth | Venus | Bull |
| Gemini | May 21 – June 21 | Masculine | Air | Mercury | Twins |
| Cancer | June 21 – July 2 | Feminine | Water | Moon | Crab |
| Leo | July 22 – August 23 | Masculine | Fire | Sun | Lion |
| Virgo | August 23 – September 23 | Feminine | Earth | Mercury | Maiden |
| Libra | September 23 – October 23 | Masculine | Air | Venus | Scales |
| Scorpio | October 23 – November 22 | Feminine | Water | Mars | Scorpion |
| Sagittarius | November 22 – December 21 | Masculine | Fire | Jupiter | Archer |
| Capricorn | December 21 – January | Feminine | Earth | Saturn | Sea-Goat |

| | | | | | |
|---|---|---|---|---|---|
| | 20 | | | | |
| Aquarius | January 20 – February 18 | Masculine | Air | Saturn | Water-Bearer |
| Pisces | February 18 – March 20 | Feminine | Water | Jupiter | Fish |

# ELEMENTAL MAGIC

The natural elements that are involved here have a large place in the world of Wicca and magic. Similar to how the placement of the stars can affect outcomes, we can predict the behavior of certain things based on their association with the elements. For example, crystals and gemstones that are associated with water are more likely to be used for healing.

While most people know of the four classical elements, Wicca believes in a fifth element that begins where the other four connect. This element is called Aether, meaning spirit. Use of the elements helps keep our practice directly in line with nature. The elements can metaphorically represent emotional and spiritual characteristics as well as the literal connection to nature.

*Air* dominates the aspect of magic that revolves around visualization. Air is a masculine element that is associated with the Eastern direction. Air represents intelligence and mental faculties, psychic abilities, imagination, ideas, the mind, dreams, and inspiration. Associated with the spring, some symbols of Air include the wind, the sky, the breeze, feathers, breath, clouds, herbs, and some flowers. Wind instruments such as the flute may be used to channel Air energy.

*Fire* is representative of magick itself. Fire is a masculine element that is associated with the Southern direction. Fire represents change and is the most physical and spiritual of all the elements. Ruled by passion, fire is often invoked through symbols such as candles, incense, baking, love spells, and burning objects.

*Water* represents cleansing and healing, and is a feminine element associated with the Western direction. Water is a receptive energy. Water itself can be easily enchanted and charged and holds energy from its surroundings very easily. Water is a dynamic representation of the subconscious emotional world, the soul, and wisdom.

*Earth* represents strength and is a feminine element associated with the Northern direction. Earth is manifested in abundance, wealth, prosperity. Rituals invoking the Earth element often involve burying an object to infuse it with strong energy promoting good fortune in finance.

*Aether* is a universal element representative of the spirit world and individual spiritual entities. Aether is the element present in some form in all things (see Animism later in this chapter). Associated with The Horned God and The Triple Goddess, Aether connects all natural things and allows the world to exist in a careful harmonious balance.

## ANIMISM: THE SOUL OF THE WORLD

*Animism* is a religious belief system that holds the value that every thing on earth, including inanimate natural objects, has a soul or a distinct spiritual essence. The title comes from the Latin *anima* which means "spirit", "breath", and "life". Animism perceives all natural things to be "alive" in the sense of having Aether, the spirit of the universe within.

It is the belief that all things of nature, sticks, rocks, animals (including humans), clouds, the wind, all these things are interconnected. The world feels the effect of the loss of any natural thing, and the balance must be maintained.

Animism was originally an ancient Indigenous belief -- that is, it was held by a large number of First Nations and Native American tribes. Wiccans often intermingle practices with First Nations religious practices because of their shared respect for the natural world. Animism is recognized as the oldest known world religion, although of course it was not an organized religion as we know today.

Those who believe in Animism today are almost always religiously pacifist, refusing to harm or kill any other being or object that contains spirit. In this way we preserve the balance, respect our place in nature, and learn to live in harmony with our environment.

Those who do not practice pacifism may choose to engage with this balance directly by hunting and gathering. Living off the land is a different approach that puts one in the middle of that balance. It teaches one how to maintain that harmony while facing the reality that, as humans, we must consume natural things to maintain our own lives.

Whether a hunter, gatherer, omnivore, or vegan, all Animists choose to honor that which they take from nature in some say. It could be in the form of a ritual, perhaps honoring the kills of the hunt before consumption or having special sacrificial rites to honor the spirits.

Nature is also honored during every Wiccan festival, but Harvest festivals in particular aim to acknowledge and give thanks for the natural blessings we receive that allow us to continue to exist in harmony with the world around us.

# TAROT: READING THE MIRROR

Many entire books could be and have been written about the subject of divination via Tarot. Tarot cards first began being used in recorded history for divination purposes in the 18th century in European countries like France and Italy.

However, many occult authors trace the unwritten history of Tarot back to ancient Egypt or ancient Kabbalah practices. There are many different styles of Tarot readings, including those from French, Celtic, and Kabbalistic backgrounds

Tarot isn't meant to be a tool to exactly read the future, either. Tarot is simply a way to measure the forces at work on the current circumstances. The outcome is in control of the seeker. The goal of Tarot is to guide the seeker and advise them of the cosmic energies at work. .

In fact, the best way to think about Tarot is a reflection of the self. The cards contain imagery that has been meaningful to humankind for centuries, and which are ingrained in what psychologist Carl Jung would call our unconscious. The cards tell a story about cosmic forces, but the cards also help us learn about ourselves in how we understand the stories the cards tell.

Tarot has 4 suits which vary by the region the cards come from. Each suit has 14 cards, nd there is an additional 21-card trump suit and a single card known as The Fool.. There are major and minor arcana elements in every suit, though the minor arcana are considered optional for readings by some practitioners. The major arcana consists of the Trump cards and The Fool, while the minor arcana is made up of the ten pip and four court cards in every deck.

The major Arcana has 22 cards, each which represents a step in a journey from The Fool's ignorance to finding wisdom and unity within the universe. Because these cards represent a progression, it can help a reader to understand this progression -- that is, where each card comes from and where it goes.

The minor Arcana suits are Swords, Cups, Wands, and Pentacles. Pulling a Sword card usually means something interpretative of your inner thoughts, your words, or your actions. The Cups generally represent feelings, inspiration, and creativity. Wands typically have to do with spirituality and energy. Finally, Pentacles are drawn to indicate something about money, material things, or stability.

The minor Arcana is more specific and not as big-picture as the major Arcana cards in the deck. The elements are also represented by the minor Arcana. Wands are fire, Cups are water, Swords are air, and Pentacles are earth.

Some Tarot readers allow cards to be drawn upside down, which changes the meaning to an inverse one. However, many Tarot readers, from beginners to experienced diviners, prefer to play only upright Arcana cards.

Tarot typically involves two people - a querent, who is posing a question to the cards, and a reader whose job it is to interpret the meaning of the cards. The querent may choose to disclose their question or keep it to themselves. A skilled reader doesn't need to know the question to read the cards.

However, as you may know, sometimes the reader is also the querent. If this is the case, the reading becomes a little different, because the cards represent people differently. A well-practiced reader will notice patterns over long periods of times in the layouts of the cards; there may be one or several cards that the reader begins to associate with themselves or others because that card appears often to represent that person.

If the imagery speaks directly to you, that intuition is recommended to be followed rather than just using the standard imagery interpretations. The cards are intending to speak directly to the reader and the seeker, so anything personal is no coincidence. Let the cards have your own voice!

The cards are pulled in some order, referred to as a spread. Maybe a one-card draw to see how your day will go, or a three-card spread asking the universe about your crush. The cards should always be read in context with other cards pulled. The positioning of the cards may also be significant, especially in Celtic and Kabbalistic card patterns. Ask yourself, how did this card work with the last card I drew?

Many Wiccans keep a log of their readings in a journal. This journal may be very thorough, writing which cards were drawn, what imagery was important, what feelings were evoked, who was doing the reading and the seeking, and how one feels about the reading. This helps the Tarot to act as a mirror to the soul of the interpreter. It allows beginners to learn more efficiently, and experienced readers to keep track of their energy.

## CONCLUSION

Wiccan practices, by nature, vary widely. There are, however, some commonly held beliefs, as we have covered, as well as festivals that most Wiccans observe. Wiccans who practice without magic celebrate the Sabbats throughout the Wheel of the Year and focus on gratitude to Mother Earth. Wiccans who practice magic still adhere to this nature-based orientation, focusing on the elements and the stars in their Craft. We can even interpret the forces of nature through divination and channel them through spells and magickal items.

The next chapter will focus on another vital component of Wiccan belief and practice, which is deity worship.

# CHAPTER 3 WICCAN DEITIES AND

# THE AFTERLIFE

Wicca is a religion that predates Christianity, so the form of worship may be unfamiliar to many. Wiccans worship specific deities within a pantheon. These Gods or Goddesses may be worshipped in hopes of advancing some cause, or a God or Goddess may "choose" a Wiccan to worship them by sending them signs.

Who you worship and how is completely your choice in Wicca. The goal is to have the most natural relationship possible, to feel intimacy with the Divine influences that surround us all. During turning points in a Wiccan's spiritual life, a new Divinity may call to them. Some Wiccans feel that a certain deity has chosen them, rather than the other way around.

There are a few distinct patterns amongst Wiccans when it comes to belief and worship of deities. More traditional Wiccans, like Gardnerian Wiccans, are polytheists who believe in two "parts" of a universal God, a male part and a female part.

Other Wiccans subscribe to polytheism, where they believe in and sometimes worship multiple Gods from a wide range of mythologies and pantheons. Celtic, Greek, Egyptian deities -- polytheists are looking to connect with deities that appear to them naturally, no matter where their lore is originally from.

Still other Wiccans consider their worship to fall *within* Abrahamic tradition; they may believe in monotheism, or they may engage in the worship of female Abrahamic figures such as Mary. Wiccans may have vastly different interpretations of traditional scriptures, and may be considered heretics by mainstream society.

## DUOTHEISM: THE HORNED GOD AND THE TRIPLE GODDESS

Those who believe in The Horned God and the Triple Goddess are considered to be *duotheistic*, meaning they believe in a dual entity of God; the male and the female. Many Wiccans feel this explains the balance in the universe, as well as the conflicts where male and female fail to harmonize.

The Horned God represents the unity "between the Divine and animals", man being included in the definition of animals. The horns represent the dualistic nature of The Horned God. He is night and he is day, summer and winter. The two horns added to the triple aspect of the Goddess are often mapped as the five points of a pentagram.

The Horned God is connected with the forest, and is seen very much as a protector of the Goddess and all her sacred children. As duality demands, he both gives life and takes souls from the world with death. He is known as a loving God who guards creation.

The Triple Goddess, completing the duotheistic belief system, represents all Divine Feminine aspects of the universe. She is most often symbolized by the moon and the ocean. The Triple Goddess gets her name from the three stages of a woman's life: The Maiden, The Mother, and The Crone. Of course this is a very ancient tradition that no longer applies universally to all women, but regardless the Triple Goddess is a representation of all the positive and negative attributes of being a woman.

The Maiden represents enchantment and youth. This is a time of purity and new beginnings. The Greek Goddess Persephone is most often associated with The Maiden.

The Mother represents fertility, power, and stability. The Mother is the ultimate creator, the giver of life, the nurturing one. In Greek myth, Demeter is associated as the Mother, a compassionate and selfless giver.

Repose and wisdom are attributes of The Crone, along with the status of being an elder. Wiccans revere their elders, as they have had much more experience in interpreting signs, interacting with spirits, and creating effective rituals. The Greek Goddess Hecate is known as The Crone, with the satisfaction of a lifetime of knowledge.


## POLYTHEISTIC PRACTICES


Other modern Wiccans are polytheists. This means that they *believe* that there are many or at least multiple deities. It doesn't mean they necessarily worship more than one deity, however; many Wiccans dedicate their practice to one or a few select Gods or Goddesses with whom they feel a special spiritual connection.

Wiccans draw deities from the lore of several different societies, including ancient Greek and Roman pantheons, along with pre-Christian European deities such as Norse myths or The Horned God. Wiccans may also spiritually access Egyptian and Hindu Gods and Goddesses.

Some Wiccans connect spiritually with their deities without naming them because their goal is to channel whoever is close and present. Other Wiccans, on the other hand, find that channeling a particular God or Goddess using certain ritual objects like candles, incense, and crystals is more effective for them. We will discuss how to begin channeling deities in Chapter 5.


## HELLENISTIC WICCA: THE PANTHEON OF OLYMPUS


Hellenistic Wiccans are those who include the Gods and Goddesses from Greco-Roman mythology in their worship and practice. Greek and Roman imagery has been so ubiquitous in our society and culture that many feel it is part of the heritage of all Wiccans. Because of this constant exposure to these myths, some Wiccans feel more strongly connected to this pantheon than to others.

Looking at the pantheon of deities from Greek and Roman myth might seem a little overwhelming. But the pantheon is very compatible with Wicca. This is because each God or Goddess is associated with something in the natural world. Indeed, many of the Gods and Goddesses exist to explain the phenomenon of the natural world around us.

The "main" Greek deities are even associated with planets and elements, and can be connected to astrology as well. The five classical elements actually come from Hellenistic understandings of the world. Before that time, the elements were known as the earth, sky, and sea by the Celtic occult groups.

This level of nuance is highly conducive to the individualism encouraged in Wiccan practice. Another advantage of Hellenistic Wicca is that unlike other European pantheons which have had much information lost to the ages, so much of the Greek and Roman lore remains in tact and accessible. In fact, there may be no pantheon more complete or detailed than that of Greece and Rome.

Hellenistic beliefs are compatible with the Wheel of the Year as well. Many Hellenistic Wiccans associate the story of Persephone and Demeter with the Wheel of the Year, because it explains the coming and going of the seasons. The rise and fall of Dionysus, the Hellenistic God of harvest, wine, and celebration, is also associated with the Sabbats and festivals.

The 12 most important Hellenistic deities are as follows:

1.   Jupiter/Zeus: King of the Gods, Zeus is the god of thunder and the sky.

2.   Hera/Juno: Queen of the Gods, Hera is the patron Goddess of women and femininity.

3.   Athena/Minerva: Born out of the head of Zeus, Athena is the Goddess of wisdom and strategy.

4.   Poseidon/Neptune: Often depicted with a trident, Poseidon is the God of the ocean and freshwater, earthquakes, and horses.

5.   Aphrodite/Venus: Aphrodite was born out of seafoam and is a maternal Goddess of sexuality, love, fertility, beauty, desire, and prosperity.

6.   Ares/Mars: The son of Hera, Ares is the God of war, aggression, virility, and the protector of agriculture.

7.   Apollo/Apollo: Depicted as  powerful archer, Apollo is the twin brother of the Goddess Artemis and  the God of healing, music, and truth.

8.   Artemis/Diana: Daughter of Zeus and twin of Apollo, Artemis is the Goddess of the hunt, the moon, birth, rebirth, and is a protector of women and a symbol of virginity.

9.   Hephaestus/Vulcan: The creator of the weapons of the Gods and Goddesses, Hephaestus is the God of the forge, metalwork, and volcanoes.

10.  Hestia/Vesta: Known as the sacred fire of the Vestal Virgins of Rome, Hestia is the Goddess of the hearth, the home, and the family.

11.  Hermes/Mercury: Son of Zeus and the guide of spirits in the underworld, Hermes is the God of communication, thieves, trickery, profit, and trade.

12.  Demeter/Ceres: Known as the eternal mother, Demeter is the Goddess of agriculture, grain, marriage, motherhood, and marriage.


# CELTIC RECONSTRUCTIONIST WICCA


Many Gardnerian Wiccans use Celtic elements in their Craft. Other Wiccans who don't identify with a tradition may also choose this path. The founder of Wicca included many Celtic influences in his original rituals and belief system, and many who believe in the traditional ways laid out by Gardner have chosen to preserve these influences.

The Celtic Reconstruction movement, associated with Neo-Druidism, is an attempt to recreate ancient Celtic practices with as much historical and spiritual accuracy as possible. Celtic traditions have survived through folklore and songs, as well as through prayers passed down through generations.

Unlike other Wiccans, Celtics believe in the Three Elements: the Land, the Sea, and the Sky. Fire is viewed as a force of inspiration which unites the three realms, and not an element in and of itself.

Celtic Wiccans are focused on interacting with the Otherworld, and use divination and offerings to connect with the ancestral spirits of the land. Offerings include food, drink (usually alcohol), and art. Most Celtic Wiccans maintain altars to honor their patron spirits and deities, and in this tradition it is most common to place the altar outside. Ideally the altar would be near a well or a stream, or some naturally occurring water.,

Some important Celtic deities include:

1.  Brighid, The Goddess of the Irish Hearth. Revered as the Goddess of the hearth and the home, Brighid is also a Goddess of prophecy and divination. Brighid is the Triple Goddess in modern Wiccan tradition.

2.  Cailleach, Queen of Winter. Sometimes known as the hag, Cailleach is the bringer of storms. Known as the Dark Mother of winter, Cailleach is also known for taking part in creation.

3.  Cernunnos, Wild God of the Forest. Representative of the Horned God in modern Wicca, Cernunnos is the god of masculinity and fertility.

4.  Cerridwen, The Keeper of the Cauldron. A Welsh Goddess, Cerridwen brews the cauldron of the underworld that is the source of ideas and inspiration.

5.  The Dagda, The Irish Father God. Legend tells that the Dagda caused himself to lose his own powers. He is the father of the other Gods and Goddesses of the Celtic pantheon.

6.  Herne, God of the Wild Hunt. An ancient English God, Herne is considered the God of the common people, as well as the God of vegetation and hunting. Herne is celebrated in the fall, when the deer go into rut.

7.  Lugh, Master of Skills. Honored during the harvest festival of Lammas, Luch is the God of craftsmanship, blacksmithing, and artisans.

8.  Rhiannon, the Welsh Goddess of Horses. Famed for her intelligence, Rhiannon is a Goddess of wealth and charity.

9.	Taliesin, Chief of Bards. Interestingly enough, Taliesin is a real documented person who has been elevated to the status of a minor Celtic God. He is the patron of poets and musicians.

# KEMETIC PANTHEON

Kemetic or Egyptian Wicca has a strong focus on the moon. Esbats are important events for them, and they gather in large groups to celebrate the moon as a community. These congregations are called temples rather than covens in this tradition.

The most important God in the Egyptian pantheon for Wiccans is Ra, the ancient God of the sun. During the day, Ra exists in the Overworld creating the sunlight and is depicted as a falcon with a sun disk around the head. At night, some legends say that Ra goes to the Underworld, and transforms to have the head of a ram, the horns representing the duality of day and night.

Ra is believed to originally been united as one being with Horus, the God of the sky. Together they made all of creation by speaking all creatures into existence using the secret names of their souls. Ra split off to rule over every domain: the sky, the earth, and the underworld.

Other important deities of this pantheon include:

1.	Amounet is the Goddess of fertility and motherhood.

2.	Anubis is the God of the dead and the process of preserving the body through embalming.

3.	Atum is a deity that switches between male and female, and is considered to be the creator of Egypt. He rose from the waters of chaos to become the first God, who created the rest of the Egyptian Gods.

4.	Bast is a Goddess of protection with the head of the cat. Originally the protector of the Pharaoh, she is gentle but a vicious enemy for those who threaten people under her protection.

5.  Hathor is the Egyptian Goddess of happiness, and was considered to be the mother of the Pharaoh. In modern Wiccan practice she is worshipped as the mother of the home and domesticity.

6.  Horus is the God who protects the Pharaoh, but was also considered to be incarnated in the Pharaoh. Horus lost an eye in battle, and since then the Eye of Horus has been an important Egyptian symbol of protection.

7.  Isis is the mother of Horus. She is a Goddess of protection and maternal love and is often depicted nursing the infant Horus.

8.  Ma'at is the daughter of Ra and the Egyptian Goddess of happiness, love, and justice.

9.  Nun is the eldest of the Egyptian Gods. Before achieving form as a God, Nun existed as the primordial waters of chaos. He is the God of pre-creation.

10. Osiris is the God of the underworld, death, and the dead.

# Norse Pantheon

Norse mythology is rich with dragons, giants, elves, dwarves vikings, and more. Though many details are lost to the ages, the tradition still lives on in Wiccan practice.

The ancient Norse folk were at times severe, but often playful as well. This playful nature is often lost in the Wiccan revival of Norse folklore and worship, traded for a focus on the warrior spirit. However, it is important to remember that the Norse ancestors weren't all kings and warriors seasoned from battle. The majority of them spent their lives performing difficult, physically demanding work and enduring cold, bitter winters. In remembering the truth about their lives, some Wiccans choose to honor their memory by engaging with the Norse pantheon.

Norse myth was transmitted through oral tradition, and by the time any of it was written down the area had already been dominated by Christians. There are two holy texts that preserve Norse legend, but they were written by Snorri

Sturlason in the 1300s after he had already been converted to Christianity. Sturlason knew that if he wrote anything the church deemed as blasphemy, he could be sentenced to death. Thus, much of the true spirit of Norse religion has been lost to time.

The Eddas contain the words of the High One, a God known as Odin who is proclaimed as the "AllFather". The values of the Eddas include truth, honor, and a moral code based on loyalty. It is written that one should protect one's own family and possessions and retaliate severely against those who betray you. The Eddas also teaches about the importance of physical and mental strength.

There are nine Nordic worlds, which are held by the branches and roots of Yggdrasil, the tree of the world. Each realm houses different beings, such as animals (including humans), Giants, and Divinities. The Norse also believe in Ragnarok, or the day of destruction.

The Norse Gods and Goddesses include:

1.  Odin is the Father of all Gods and humans. Often depicted wearing a floppy hat or a winged helm, Odin is a warrior God known for wisdom, magick, wit, and knowledge. Though he is known as a literal warrior, Odin also represents mental warfare, considering his cerebral qualities. Odin is associated with the astrological sign Sagittarius.

2.  Thor is the son of Odin and the God of thunder, lightning, and strength. Thor is typically shown wielding his mighty hammer, Mjollnir. Rugged and powerful, Thor guards Asgard, the realm of the Gods. Thor is linked with the astrological sign Leo.

3.  Freya is a Goddess known for love and beauty, but she is also a hyper-intelligent warrior. Freya guides the souls she chooses that are lost in battle to Valhalla, the Norse heaven. She and her twin brother Freyr are connected to the astrological sign Gemini.

4.  Freyr, twin of Freya, is known as the God of the Elves. Freyr is a God of virility and fertility. His boar is a sacred symbol that is said to bring the dawn.

5.  Tyr is the God of the ancient wars and the lawmaker for the Gods. Tyr is invoked to bring about justice and right action. Tyr used to be the leader of the Norse pantheon, but was replaced by Odin. There are no record that explain why this transition occurred. Tyr is associated with the astrological sign Libra

6.  Loki is a trickster God, known for his acts of chaos. While he challenges the structure and rules of Asgard, his antics are necessary to bring about the change the world needs. Loki has demonic elements, and is associated with the astrological sign Aries.

7.  Heimdall is a handsome God with golden teeth. His role is to guard the rainbow path that leads to the realm of the Gods. He holds the signal horn that is blown to warn the Gods of Ragnarok. Heimdall is linked to the astrological sign Aquarius.

8.  Skadi is the Goddess of winter and the hunt. She is a Goddess of judgment, vengeance, and righteous anger. It is she who delivers Loki's banishment to the underworld. Skadi is represented by the astrological sign Capricorn.

# ABRAHAMIC WICCA

While some might see it as a contradiction or heresy, there are followers of the three Abrahamic religions that also identify with and practice Wicca. Abrahamic Wiccans believe that the one Abrahamic God controls all of existence, including the stars that guide astrology. An Abrahamic Wiccan would argue that if you pull a card from a tarot deck, the Abrahamic God controlled the outcome of which card appeared. Thus, Wicca can interpret the signs sent by the Abrahamic God through the universe.

Though all of the Abrahamic religions center around the same God, described by different prophets, there is much nuance and difference in the way they worship, practice, and perceive God. They also use different central religious texts.

All Abrahamic Wiccans believe in emulating the behavior of the prophets of God. Christians additionally focus on living a life mimicking the path of Jesus and his disciples. Muslims imitate the life of Muhammad, and Wiccans often include the behavior of the wives of Muhammad to provide feminine balance.

Many Abrahamic Wiccan women choose to cover their hair as a sign of devotion and remembrance of God. Jewish women honor God in this way by wearing *tichel,* which are wraps that go around the back of the head but do not cover the neck or face. Christian women often wear veils made of lace, or veils that wrap loosely around the head to show the hair but not the neck, in imitation of Mother Mary. Muslim Wiccan women wear the *hijab,* a veil that covers all of the hair as well as the chest and neck, or a *niqab* which also covers the face.

Jewish Wiccans focus on the Tanakh, or the Hebrew Bible as their central texts. This is known by Christians as The Old Testament. For Jewish Witches, God is known by a respectful title HaShem, which means simply "The Name". This is because outside of prayer and ritual environments, the names of HaShem are considered to be too holy to speak aloud. HaShem is called Adonai when called upon in prayer, but also has seven names which reveal more about the nature of the Divine.

A Jewish Wiccan would be most likely to practice Kabbalah, or the ancient art of Jewish mysticism. The Zohar is the book which explains how to begin to understand the complex and multilayered realms of Kabbalah. Kabbalah tries to understand the secret meanings of the Torah, often by using complicated numerology. Hebrew letters are also numbers, so the Torah can be interpreted by examining the patterns therein.

The most traditional Kabbalistic Jewish Wiccans believe that one cannot even begin to fathom the truths of Kabbalah until one has reached the age of 40. However, there are Kabbalistic tarot spreads and other methods of accessing the knowledge of Kabbalah before this coming of age occurs.

The Bible is the main holy text for Christian Wiccans, though The Old Testament is important for context as well.

Christian Wiccans often venerate the saints as well as the Virgin Mary. Mary represents the Divine Feminine. Calling from Wiccan influences, Mary represents all at once The Maiden, The Mother, and The Crone, being pure, maternal, and wise. This balances the trinity of God, which is the Father, the Son, and the Holy Spirit.

Christian Wiccans celebrate both Christian holidays and the festivals of the Wheel of the Year, mixing elements of both belief systems into each holiday. Christmas and Easter, as they are celebrated, actually already incorporate many pagan rituals such as tree-decorating and fertility symbols (e.g. eggs, rabbits).

There is also a large focus on returning to the roots of Christianity. This means being highly educated on the facts about the life of Jesus of Nazareth and what He stood for instead of taking someone else's word for it. Many Wiccans feel that Christianity has been wrongly warped from its original intentions and used as a device for war and division when it preaches about peace and unity.

The holy book of Muslims is called the Qu'ran. Qu'ran means "recitation" in Arabic, and recitation of the Qu'ran is extremely important to all Muslims. It is said that Allah gave the Qu'ran to the humans and the djinn (spirits), but not to the Angels. Thus, whenever one recites Qu'ran, the Angels draw in close to listen. You are encouraged to greet the Angels who peek over your shoulders when you finish your recitation.

There are different sects of Islam just as there are for every large religion. Most Wiccan Muslims are in a sect called *Sufism*. Sufism is Islamic mysticism. Islamic mysticism focuses on the power of trance and meditation, worshipping the divine feminine, and worship through music and dance. Whereas most Muslims harshly condemn magick, Sufis defy labels and many don't self-identify even as Sufis. Sufis believe in full capacity for spiritual growth in all directions.

## *WICCAN AFTERLIFE*

After all that discussion about divinity, it seems only appropriate to address what Wiccans believe about the great beyond. While Abrahamic Wiccans may follow the afterlife beliefs of their own traditions, the majority of Wiccans believe in reincarnation and a realm called the Summerland.

## THE CIRCLE OF REINCARNATION

Pulling from beliefs that predate the Abrahamic religions, most Wiccans don't believe in heaven or hell. These concepts did not exist in ancient religions, though they did have ideas about what happens after death. Many Wiccans believe that when you die, you are reborn again into the cycle of the cosmos.

Just as Wiccans believe in the Wheel of the Year and the cycles of the moon, reincarnation is just another cycle in the universe. We are born, we live, we die, and we are reborn again. Many witches believe in a karmic system, where what one does in this life will have a ripple effect through one's coming lives. Because of this, Wiccans take their actions very seriously, and do their best to lead kind, compassionate lives.

Wiccans believe we are put on this Earth to constantly be in a state of self-improvement. If you've ever known a Wiccan, you probably know there's a large focus to constantly be learning, reading, and discussing, as well as reevaluating ideals. This is often called the Great Work.

According to Wiccan legend, we are gifted more than one life in order to learn all that we can possibly know about nature and the cosmos. One life is not sufficient for this to occur. Each ner lifetime encompasses a set of lessons, and the universe has such a vast variety of lessons to teach each and every one of us. Indeed, each soul is unique and needs to learn different lessons at different times.

Once one has perfected this knowledge, after many, many lifetimes, one is released from the cycle of reincarnation and enters the Summerland, which is the topic of the next section. Apart from being an escape from reincarnation, the Summerland is also the place where the soul rests between incarnations. This is often a time to reunite with loved ones from all our different lives, should they happen to be in the Summerland at the same time.

For Wiccans, death is just another step in the eternal dance of the balance of the universe. The soul itself has no name, no gender, no race, no age, and is not a physical thing. It is a spark reflected from the deities, whichever one might follow. While the body may die, the soul will always live on; it is immortal.

When the soul visits the Summerland between incarnations, it is not a time of judgment but rather a time for weighing what has been gained and learned, and what lesson the soul will need to continue to grow in the next life.

The soul is able to see which lessons in the previous lives were heeded, and which were ignored. The soul reviews the previous life, with the insight of other spirits and deities that exist in the Summerland.

Some witches are able to access information about their past lives. There are several methods through which this can be done. Some witches receive information about past lives through dreams. These dreams may feature a guide, usually a spirit or deity, that shows the witch visions of the past. Spirits or deities may choose to do this if past knowledge will benefit the witch in the lessons of their current incarnation.

Others work to enter a trance state where this information is more readily accessible. It takes a great deal of discipline and practice to use this method. Trance work is part of the shamanistic tradition, and is not to be taken lightly. Witches should remember the persecution of witches that has existed for millenia, and be prepared to face some very difficult images and information. This kind of trance work is known as *journeying*.

So why would a witch want to seek information from a past life? Many witches believe that the key to understanding the deeper problems they face, mentally, emotionally, spiritually, and physically, lies in having an understanding of who we used to be. If a witch has issues making the same mistakes over and over in their current life, it could be a sign that they need to get in touch with their past lives to gain insight.

Because of their belief in reincarnation, Wiccans do not fear death. Wiccans don't view death as a release into oblivion, but rather as a door to birth and renewal. In your life, you meet your loved ones from past lives and get to know them again fresh, as strangers. This helps you to know the souls of your friends and family more completely, to form stronger and stronger bonds over the course of your various incarnations.

Some Wiccans believe in "soul groups" that gather and reincarnate together. These souls are deeply interconnected, and their lessons and knowledge-seeking requires every soul for completion. Some covens believe they have practiced together through many generations of incarnation.

Souls that have finished incarnating that remain in the summerland help the younger souls who still have things to learn. Within the Summerland there exists the Hall of Ancestors, where our ancestral souls who have finished incarnating feast and celebrate the beauty and joy of all they have learned and lived. These ancestors and spirits that remain in the Summerlands can be invoked or called upon for guidance by Wiccans in the mortal realm.

Because Wiccans believe in animism, and thereby believe in the souls of animals and other life forms, some Wiccans also believe animal souls enter and are reborn through the Summerland. Animals are reincarnated as other animals, and complete their own spiritual journey that human beings cannot fully comprehend. For example, a dog may have been a lion in a past life.

## *THE SUMMERLAND*

The Summerland is known by many names. Some call it Land of the Faerie, the Shining Land, the Otherworld, or Land of the Young. The Summerland is where the soul rests between reincarnations, and where a soul receives its final rest once the soul has completed its quest for knowledge in the mortal, earthly realms.

The concept of the Summerland is drawn, again, from the Old Religions. It is similar to the Celtic concept of Avalon. It also draws elements from the Roman and Greek concept of the afterlife, Elysium.

The Summerland is a realm, just like the one we inhabit during our lives, except it is much less dense than the realm in which living creatures dwell. This realm is neither heaven nor a hell-like underworld. There are two typical ways that the Summerland is envisioned by Wiccans.

The first way that the Summerland is visualized is a land of eternal abundance and summer. Wiccan souls in the Summerland escape the cycle of the seasons which include the loss and emptiness of winter, the rebirth and growth of spring, and the harvest of autumn. The Summerland from this perspective is a place with flowing, beautiful grassy fields where the gentle breeze soothes the soul after a long journey. There are peacefully flowing rivers. The soul finally unifies with all that is natural.

The second way the Summerland is conceptualized is a place without form. Souls interact directly, without bodies, communicating through and with the forces of the universe. The energies of souls are intertwined with the highest energies, those of the deities. Here one has a chance to unify with the identities of the celestial beings.

No matter which way one envisions the Summerland, its purpose is to prepare the soul for its new life. The process ages the soul in reverse; it becomes younger and younger until it is ready again to inhabit a new blessed infant. However, different souls may take more or less time to complete this process. That is to say, a soul that is 85 years old will not necessarily take only 85 years to grow young again.

## CONCLUSION

As you might be able to tell by the wide variety of belief systems, Wicca is not a prescriptive religion. Wicca is a religion that encourages all seekers to find their own paths, and judgment from other Wiccans is highly frowned upon. There is not a right or wrong way to be a Wiccan. It is all about pursuing what calls to you, as long as that path does no harm to others.

# CHAPTER 4: WICCAN TOOLS

## ALTARS AND ALTAR TOOLS

Wiccans maintain an altar. An *altar* is is a sacred space cultivated by a Wiccan for meditation, prayer, offerings, spells, and divination. The altar can also be a space to connect with and worship deities. Altars are decorated with tools, crystals, art, and other things to make them unique and to help them channel the desired energies. Some Wiccans maintain multiple altars for different purposes.

The altar is the heart of one's sacred space. It is an area of concentrated energy, the seat of a Wiccan's worship. While in most organized religions the altar is found at the front of a congregation, inaccessible to the congregants, the altar in Wicca is very personal. The altar is not shared with a whole community; it is a place for private worship and solitary devotion to the sacred.

Building your first altar can seem daunting, but it is an opportunity to create something completely unique. For some it is so intimidating that it is put off.

Your altar doesn't have to mimic anyone else's or have significance to anyone except for you. As long as the items on your altar are meaningful to you, that is all that matters.

Conversely, over-excitement can lead to a crowded altar covered with distracting trinkets that will only serve to collect dust. You want your altar to contain useful things. Altars are dynamic as well; what may be useful on your altar at first may eventually have fully served its purpose and need to be replaced as your beliefs and Craft develop.

Before we look at the different types of altars, it is important to understand the tools of the altar and their purposes, significances, and uses. The four main tools of the altar are the athame, the wand, the chalice, and the pentacle, each representing a different element. These four tools appear in the minor arcana of tarot, known as Swords, Cups, Pentacles, and Wands in the deck. The next sections will cover other important tools as well.

Don't worry about collecting all the tools as a beginner. The point is to learn about these tools and understand their uses. No tools are necessary to practice Wicca, but as you develop your practice you're likely to begin accruing them.

## ATHAMES

An athame is a special dagger used for magickal rituals. The athame often is double-edged, with a pointed, sharp tip. Athames should be used with great care to prevent harm during use. Respect the athame as you would any other kind of knife. The handle of the athame is often inscribed with symbols or sigils. These carvings can vary depending on which tradition the practitioner is a part of.

The purpose of the athames are not to cut things, but rather to direct energy during the ritual. Cutting is considered a mundane task, and athames are reserved for the sacred. The athame represents the fire element. It is used to cast circles by outlining their circumference. The athame wards off negative energies and spirits during magickal work.

## BOLINES

A boline is a ritual knife used for more mundane tasks than the athame. Traditionally the blade is one-sided and straight, but it is becoming more and more common to find them in a crescent shape to invoke the moon and the Triple Goddess. The boline has a white handle rather than a black one, and is usually smaller than an athame. The boline is used to cut herbs and cord, and to carve wands and candles.

## PENTACLES

While the pentacle and the pentagram are related, they are not the same. To use the words interchangeably is incorrect, and it is important to know the difference.

The pentagram symbol is a five-pointed star contained in a circle. It is a type of talisman and can also be worn as an amulet. The five points on the pentagram represent many things. They represent the five elements. For Wiccans who worship The Horned God and The Triple Goddess, the five points also represent the two horns of the God and the three forms of the Goddess.

However, a ritual pentacle is different from the simple symbol pentagram. The pentacle is drawn as a pentagram, but also includes other writing. A ritual pentagram is often the centerpiece of the altar. It can be used to summon spirits or energies. The pentagram can be made from many natural materials, such as wood or paper. Within the pentagram, the words and symbols of whatever is being summoned are drawn.

## CHALICES

A chalice is a cup used for ritual purposes, often resembling a goblet. A chalice my be filled with wine, whiskey, beer, water, or a number of other fluids with magickal properties depending on what the ritual is for. The ancient Romans would drink from chalices at banquets and feasts, and at the dawn of Christianity chalices were used for ritual purposes.

The chalice represents the element of water, and represents the womb. If one worships a female deity, it could represent the womb of that deity and be used to encourage fertility. The base of the chalice represents the physical world. The stem of the chalice symbolizes the connection between the mind, the body, and the spirit. The rim is that from which we receive spiritual energy, if the chalice is used to drink from.

When used in combination with an athame, the chalice and the athame together represent the feminine womb of the Goddess and the masculine phallus of the God coming together to create.

## WANDS

A wand is a thin, straight carved piece of wood, ivory, metal, or even crystal. The wand is meant to be hand-held. Originally, wands were supposed to stretch from the tip of the middle finger to the elbow, but as tradition has evolved wands have become smaller. Wand traditions trace back to ancient Egypt, where wands were buried in tombs for souls to use in the afterlife. The Hellenistic God Hermes/Mercury is also depicted as having used a wand.

Wands are commonly carved from wood of sacred trees, such as willow, elder, and oak. However, with new technology wands can be made from many materials. Some modern wands are made entirely of crystal or have crystal tips attached.

While the most effective wands are handcrafted, store-bought wands also work if you feel a connection with them.

## CANDLES

Candles are a primary tool for Wiccans, and their different colors are used for different purposes. During a ritual they are placed at the four corners of the ritual circle to represent the presence of the four elements Fire, Wind, Earth, and Water (Aether is represented by the practitioners themselves).

Candles can be consecrated and charged for use by cleansing and anointing them with concentrated essential oils. Always do your research before using an oil, because some are more flammable than others, and you don't want an out of control blaze on your hands. Many Wiccans also sprinkle dried herbs over the candles to invoke their properties.

The colors of the candles are very important to for rituals and spells. Luckily, candles can often be found for low prices at your local dollar store, or in bulk online. Below is a brief review of the various candle colors and what they represent and invoke.

White: unity; spiritual truth; strength; peace and purity; breaking curses; meditation; purification

Yellow: persuasion; creativity; confidence and charisma; improving memory and studying

Green: nature, renewal, and fertility; healing; money and prosperity; emotional soothing and balance

Pink: love and strengthening friendships; femininity; spiritual healing; warding away evil

Red: strength and vitality; power; sexuality; passion; protection; the cycle of reincarnation

Orange: strength, courage, and authority; concentration; encouragement

Blue: psychic powers and spiritual awareness; wisdom and intelligence; harmony and balance; dreams of prophecy; protection while sleeping

Purple: mysticism; ambition; inspiration and idealism; heightening psychic abilities; breaking curses

Brown: animal healing; protection of animals; attracting money; solving domestic issues; finding lost objects

Gold: masculinity; intuition; persuasion and charm; protection; gaining luck and fortune quickly

Silver: removing negativity and encouraging stability; neutrality; developing psychic ability

Black: loss, grief, disappointment, and sadness; depression; absorbing and destroying evil and discord; protection from retribution

If a spell calls for a candle color you don't currently have, white candles are often used as a neutral acceptable replacement. It helps to carve a sigil in the candle to endow it with the energy of the colored candle you are replacing.

# INCENSE

Incense is another important tool for many Wiccans. Incense is a substance, usually found in the form of a stick of infused herbs, which can be burned to release a fragrant smoke. Thought to have originally been used by Egyptians, the practice spread far and wide, adopted by Romans and Greeks and pagans worldwide.

Incense represents four elements at once. It is created from materials from the Earth by soaking them in Water. Then it is ignited with Fire, upon which time it wafts smoke through the Air. Some Wiccans consider its connection to Air to be the strongest, because it is an aesthetic representation of Air and helps us see the movement of the air around us.

Incense is held in a special container called a censer. This can take many forms. It could be a flat, straight piece of wood or other material upon which the ash can fall. Some witches fill a ceramic or metal cauldron with coal and burn incense within the cauldron. For certain rituals, ashes are important, so often times the ashes are saved to use in other spells and rituals.

There is an enormous variety of incense to choose from, but there are definitely types that are more commonly used. Frankincense is used to invoke masculine power and the sun. It is burned to encourage deep spirituality and purification. Myrrh is similar in function to Frankincense, but is a feminine incense that also promotes healing. Pine and Cedar incense are used to cleanse a space. Copal is also used for cleansing, but is often used specifically to cleanse objects.

Another form of incense use is the use of dried bundles of white sage. The tips of the bundles are lit, while the user holds the base where the sage is tied together with string. The user then cleanses whatever needs to be cleansed. It could be tools, or a space. It is often used to dispel negative energies and spirits from entire houses, especially when one has just moved in. This process is called *smudging*.

## TYPES OF ALTARS

One of the first steps to building your own altar is choosing what kind of altar you want. This will help you decide what should be present and what can be left out and used for other purposes.

## SHRINES

A shrine is an altar created for the purpose of venerating a deity, or less commonly for ancestor worship. A shrine is the perfect place to pray, commune with your deity, and make offerings. Making offerings, such as flowers, herbs, or alcohol, brings you closer to the deity. Offerings also encourage the deity to guide you in general, or to help you with a specific task.

Shrines are typically simple, because they are a focal point and therefore should have a clear, focused energy. A representation of the focus of the shrine is usually used, whether its a statue or a drawing or photograph. Candles are placed on the shrine to "activate" the energy of the shrine. Small decorations such as vases are good ways to keep fresh offerings present, and also a good way to remember Wiccan veneration of all that is natural.

Really, that is all that is necessary for a shrine. Simplicity is the name of the game with this type of altar. Of course, you can add stones, crystals, and other things that channel or remind you of the subject of your worship. You should carefully consider what you add, though, to prevent your shrine from looking like a New Age flea market display.

During Samhain, ancestral shrines are much more elaborate. Ancestral shrines are decorated with photos of the ancestor, as well as personal belongings of theirs. Seasonal decorations such as apples, pumpkins, and root vegetables are often piled high as offerings to the departed. For a Samhain shrine, color is also important. Rich deep colors that represent the end of fall are used such as black, gold, and burgundy.

## RITUAL ALTARS

A ritual altar is more elaborately done because it includes the tools necessary to perform the ritual. Ritual altars are used for occasions such as Esbats or festivals. A full ritual altar often includes an athame, wand, cup, pentagram, and candles (often many of them in different colors).

Because of all the tools that are usually present during a full-blown ritual, these altars are usually quite large and often temporary. Ritual altars are typically constructed outdoors, where the connection with nature is strongest.

## WORKING ALTAR

A working altar is an altar that is prepared for functional, practical magickal use. While some work can be completed in a single session, other ritual sessions or spells may require you to return to the altar multiple times. Thus, these altars are often more permanent than ritual altars.

This type of altar should be extremely focused and contain no more pieces than is absolutely necessary for the work being done. Excess tools and trinkets will distract from the magickal work and divert energy to other places.

## PERSONAL ALTAR

A personal altar is more permanent, although the pieces included on the altar will change over time as your needs change. This kind of altar is often elaborately decorated with images, cloths, photos, crystals, candles, incense, and flowers. A personal altar is used to generate the desired vibrations. It can be focused on one particular energy, but in this case it does not have to be.

With any type of altar one should be cautious of clutter. Don't hold onto items that don't have meaning to you, or that have worn out their usefulness. It's easy to become attached to material things, but this is contradictory to the Wiccan path. It is not the material things a Wiccan owns that gives them power. The power comes from within. If you're having trouble with materialism, take time to enjoy nature and remember the true roots of Wicca.

# CRYSTALS

Gemstones and crystals are commonly used by Wiccans to channel certain cosmic energies in their day-to-day practices, or on special occasions. This section will teach you about what energies are held by which crystals and gemstones, and will also discuss how crystals can be used in magic.

There are a large range of purposes that crystals can be used for in magic. Crystals can be worn in jewelry to help you guide a certain vibration into your life on the go, for example. Crystals are also commonly found on the altars of many Wiccans. Whether you're looking to be more creative, be luckier in your love life, or be more in-tune with nature, there's a gemstone that will match the needs of your practice at any time in your life.

All stones can be charged, just like spells or water. Stones are great vessels for energy, and can be charged in the light of the full moon or by the bright shining sun during the day. Stones can be cleansed in a variety of ways, but some stones may be corroded by water so it is important to research the physical properties of the stone.

Cleansing a stone is often done once a month during the full moon, simply by leaving the crystals and stones out in the moonlight to refresh and rejuvenate their energies. At other times of the month, stones can be cleansed by burning cleansing herbs, most commonly sage. The stone should be held over the smoke and usually an incantation is read.

Stones associated with the element of your Astrological sign or with elements that resonate strongly with you may be easier for you to channel with, but any Wiccan can still work with any stone. Stones can also be attuned to your entire Astrological chart (e.g. using Amethyst to heal your love life if your Venus is a water sign).

## AGATE

Agate can have many unique appearances, but generally has lush gold or bronze bands rippling through this unique stones. Blues, whites, and purples are also common colors found blended into this earthy stone.

Being connected with the Earth elements and the brow chakra, Agate is a stone that helps focus the mind. It can relieve depression and give you more energy. If you're feeling down and out, and could use some stress relief, carrying agate with you, wearing it as jewelry, or placing agate on your altar are magic practices that could offer you relief.

## AMETHYST

This well-known and often-used favorite comes in a deep purple color, and is known to be associated with the Astrological sign Aquarius. This violet quartz crystal is a stone filled with water energies.

Associated with the crown of the head, amethyst is a healing stone, often used in rituals to heal anxiety or mood disorders. Amethyst can also be used to help cleanse a ritual space of negative spirits or energies that might be present, making it the perfect crystal to keep in an altar.

## BLOODSTONE

Bloodstone is usually an olive green color with brown speckles decorating it. This stone is also known for healing properties, and as a fire stone is associated with Mars and the sun.

Bloodstone is particularly useful for its fertility properties, so if you're looking to start or grow your family, or if you're intending to channel fertility for another person, this is a great option for you.

## DIAMONDS

Diamonds are a clear stone, with a foggy appearance when uncut and a very radiant, sparkly appearance when cut that catches the light from every angle. These stunning stones are associated with the Sun and fire energy.

Diamonds can be used for the classic reasons of encouraging cosmic encounters that lead to engagement and marriage, but are another great stone for the treatment of fertility issues as well. A diamond can be used to treat infertility in men or women, including treating impotence in the bedroom.

## GARNET

This burgundy stone can resemble the deep red of blood, or appear more purple. Garnet is connected with the Goddess Persephone and the fire element.

Garnets are strongly connected with moon magic, and can be charged by being left out to absorb the energy from a full moon, blue moon, blood moon, etc. This stone is tied to the complexities of a woman's body, and can be used to encourage fertility and regulate the menstrual cycle. A charged garnet will also boost other stones present at an altar.

## HEMATITE

While unknown to many outside of magic practice, hematite is a favorite amongst Wiccans. This gorgeous silver-colored stone has ties with fire and the planet Saturn.

Hematite is used for healing, and is especially potent for treating blood disorders, infections, and fevers. A protection stone, it is great to have around on you to ward off negative energy and to protect you from hostile spirits. As jewelry, this stone can increase psychic awareness and magic ability.

# JADE

Jade is a peaceful stone that is typically known for its beautiful green hue, though it comes in other colors as well. Associated with earth elements, this stone is a symbol of serenity.

Jade can be used to channel calmness, true love, and innocence. Jade is also used to balance the humors of the body in the liver and spleen.

# JASPER

Jasper has a red-brown marble color, often with flecks of white mixed in. Associated strongly with earth elements, this stone is perfect for Tauruses, Virgos, and Capricorns.

Jasper can be used in rituals to ground and center your magic and your mind, perfect for concentration when working on spells or studying. It also has healing properties, specifically good for cancer treatment. You can also place a piece under your mattress to bring an extra spark to your love life!

# LAPIS LAZULI

This stone may not be as shiny as some others, but the range of blues from light cerulean to deep royal blue make it undeniably elegant. Lapis Lazuli is often spotted or banded, depending on where the stone originally grew.

Lapis Lazuli is known to alleviate depression and soothe the mind. It is the best stone for meditation and trance exercises.

# MOONSTONE

A soft opalescent milky white, moonstone has magical connections with -- you guessed it! The moon. It also is connected with lunar deities, and the number three. Any Wiccan who is working with the number three or worships a deity involved with the number three will find use out of this brilliant stone.

This is another great stone to charge under special moon events. Because the moon is associated with femininity, this stone can be used to promote fertility as well as regulating the menstrual cycle. In terms of magical qualities, moonstone can help you get in touch with your wisdom when you need it the most. Moonstone is also great for intuition, and is the perfect stone to keep present at a tarot reading or other divination project.

## QUARTZ CRYSTAL

Quartz crystals are clear, but often have small milky flaws in them. Wiccan highly value these flaws, and for this reason a "crystal ball" should always be made from quartz rather than glass. The unique flaws in a Quartz are capable of snagging onto passing energies, which makes them useful in a spherical form or in a pendulum shape for divination.

Clear Crystal Quartz is an all-around positivity stone, and is very commonly worn in jewelry. The stone gives positive energy, general cleansing, and has gentle healing properties. It is an excellent stone for beginners who may feel overwhelmed by the energy of more powerful stones.

## ROSE QUARTZ

The Rose Quartz is a fan favorite amongst Wiccans, both for its beauty and its gentle energy. Like Quartz Crystal, Rose Quartz is valued for its flaws and the variety of patterns in which it can manifest. Rose Quartzes are a soft rosy pink. Some are more clear, while others have a pink milky swirl within them.

Rose Quartz can be used to promote happiness, for new or deeper love, to help encourage forgiveness, and to bring about peace. It is a symbol of love and healthy relationships. The love radiated by a Rose Quartz is not only love for and from others, but love for the self as well.

## TIGER'S EYE

Tiger's Eye is a warm golden stone with deep brown streaks that go all the way through the length of the stone. The gold has a very distinctive shimmer in the light, and is quite a sight to behold. Tiger's Eye is a strong stone for protection.

The main purpose of Tiger's Eye is to give oneself clarity. Tiger's Eye helps you see through illusions, and helps you to identify the truth. This stone can also help us learn inner truths about ourselves.

## TURQUOISE

Known for its striking bright blue with veins of brown, Turquoise is strongly associated with the astrological sign Sagittarius. Turquoise is another stone that promotes complete positivity. Turquoise is known for attuning to its user, focusing their energy wherever it is needed most.

This is the ultimate stone for healing. It promotes emotional, physical, mental, and spiritual well-being. It neutralizes negative energy and provides strong protection. It also promotes joy, friendship, and relaxation.

## GRIMOIRES: A WITCH'S DIARY

A *grimoire* is often simply explained as a spellbook. Indeed, grimoires are often used to collect information about how to perform spells properly for easy, quick reference and access. While you can buy one, it is encouraged to eventually move on to create your own that is specific to your needs for your practice.

Also known as a Book of Shadows, this journal contains more than just spells. This is a place where Wiccans collect all their knowledge of the Craft for easy reference. Grimoires often contain information about herbs, crystals, astrology, moon cycles, and much more. This book is a Wiccan's go-to resource for their Craft.

Because of the critical focus on nature, Wiccans are constantly learning about the world around them. This often includes having a wide range of knowledge about natural materials, their correspondences, and their uses. Any magickal information may be recorded in a grimoire.

Wiccans have widely different traditions about how to create a grimoire. Many covens have specific rules and layouts to follow. This often includes consecrating the grimoire to endow it with sacred energy, and cleansing the book of any energy it may have previously held. Some Wiccans choose to mask the information by using codes, cyphers, or symbols to prevent the grimoire from being used by others.

Your grimoire should be created following your own intuition. If you want to use symbols and codes, that's your own decision. What you choose to write in your grimoire is also done at your own discretion.

In today's modern age, many choose to create a grimoire online using any of the multitudes of journaling software available. The benefit to this method is that the grimoire would be searchable by keywords, and it could have a password protecting its contents. This option is great for having your grimoire on the go without needing a physical copy.

Many people feel discouraged by poor handwriting or less than perfect art skills, and a digital grimoire offers a creative way to collect information without needing technical crafting skills.

Another method especially good for beginners is to create a binder. This allows you to move pages around or remove them without damaging the book. You can add dividers to separate clear sections to find things easily. For those without artistic ability, this is a good option because you can create and print out your own pages to go in the grimoire. For example, you can include photos of herbs and plants to help identify them alongside information about their medicinal and magickal properties.

Finally, a grimoire can be made from a bound journal. Often, these journals are decorated with magick symbols such as the symbol of the Triple Goddess. Some like to glue small flat crystals to the front, and to press flowers and herbs between the pages.

For beginners, many experienced Wiccans recommend starting two grimoires. One is the "final" grimoire, which contains your best art and your finest handwriting. The other would be a draft of a grimoire, where messiness is allowed. This allows you to experiment with the order of your entries and practice what you would like to write and draw before making it "official". Another method of having two grimoires is to have one for day-to-day witchcraft, and one for special occasions.

The most common advice given to beginners is not to take the grimoire so seriously that you are afraid to begin. The grimoire should come naturally. It is something to enjoy and cherish, not a chore or obligation. Work at your own pace, and experiment with different methods to find out what is right for you.

# HERBS

Herbalism, or the study of the medicinal and magickal properties of herbs, is very popular amongst Wiccans. Wiccans believe herbs are not only beneficial because of their own characteristics, but also because they are endowed with the energy of the Earth. Each herb has unique uses, and Wiccans utilize them in a variety of ways.

It is important here to note that although Wiccans practice herbal remedies, this is not a replacement for professional medical treatment. It is a supplementary practice rather than a replacement for modern medicine.

Wiccans use herbs as natural remedies for minor pains and conditions, like headaches or indigestion. Many herbs can be made into teas or used to season food. Some Wiccans enjoy creating their own tea blends. Consuming an herb can also help you channel the magickal properties of that herb. For example, saffron is thought to boost creativity and is often enjoyed as a tea with a rich red hue.

Some Wiccans choose to grow their own herbs to connect with the earth and the Wheel of the Year. Many herbs can be grown indoors, if a garden is not available. Herbs are traditionally harvested in the morning, before the heat of the day sets in but after the sun has dried the dew from the plants. Harvested herbs can be used fresh in cooking, or hung upside-down to dry. Dried herbs can be used in kitchen witchery, and also can be burned in small quantities as incense.

The three most commonly used herbs in witchcraft are rosemary, thyme, and lavender. These three are considered essentials, although all herbs have their own unique values. They can be used fresh, dried, as incense, or as an essential oil. Here's what you need to know about the big three.

## *ROSEMARY*

Rosemary is associated with the Sun and the astrological sign Leo. The primary correspondences for rosemary are creativity, wisdom, vitality, healing, protection, purification, love, strength, and stress relief. Rosemary is also known to provide mental clarity and confidence.

Rosemary is an acceptable substitute for Frankincense, an herb that grows in few climates and tends to be expensive. Rosemary can also be placed under a pillow to promote new ideas and creativity. A rosemary bath provides invigoration and positive energy.

## *THYME*

Thyme is associated with Mercury and Venus, as well as the element water and the astrological signs Taurus and Libra. Thyme makes a delicious tea. The primary correspondences for thyme are beauty, courage, psychic knowledge, healing, love, and purification. Thyme is also known to be very grounding, and can help avoid conflict.

Thyme is a favorite herb of the Fae. Planting thyme in your garden or home may attract them, so be sure to keep the thyme plants healthy! Faeries can be tricksters when they're displeased.

## *LAVENDER*

Lavender is associated with the planet Mercury, the element air, and the astrological signs Gemini and Virgo. Its fragrance is very gentle and relaxing, and because of this it is often used to create "dream pillows". Dream pillows have lavender in their stuffing to help you fall asleep and to cast away bad dreams.

Lavender's primary correspondences are love, beauty, protection, relaxation, sleep, and psychic knowledge. Lavender is a lovely addition to bath water, to fully appreciate its lovely fragrance and to take time to unwind after a long day.

# FAMILIARS SPIRITS: ANIMAL COMPANIONSHIP

Recorded accounts of familiar spirits go back to the Medieval ages, and the practice itself certainly existed before it was ever written down. A familiar is an animal, usually small, that acts as a companion and spirit guide. However, almost any animal can serve as a familiar.

In Wiccan history, witches who worked with familiar spirits were severely persecuted. A familiar was speculated to be a demon or some other evil paranormal force that could shape-shift into the form of an animal. Familiars were thought to serve witches by spying for them and cursing their enemies. All familiars were assumed by Christians to be malevolent.

Witches in the Middle Ages were often ostracized, marginalized, and lonely. For this reason, many began to keep small pets around for companionship. During the witch hysteria of the Middle Ages, owning a black cat was sufficient enough reason for extensive investigation into a woman's life.

Familiars were often used as evidence in witch trials in 16th and 17th century in England and Scotland. Leviticus, the third book of the Old Testament, mentions familiar spirits by name, and calls for anyone who works with familiars to be stoned to death. Thousands of women were executed, many of them having no connection at all with Wicca.

For the modern-day witch it is a happy blessing to gain this kind of bond with an animal. Keeping a familiar is a way for witches, especially those in the city, to cultivate a rapport with nature. Animals are much more in-tune with both natural and supernatural phenomena. Animals are sensitive to weather, and will often begin to act strangely if malevolent spirits are present.

By developing a relationship with a familiar, one can strengthen psychic abilities. The familiar can act as a medium between this world and the next. If you are attuned to the body language of your pet, you can recognize when supernatural beings are nearby.

# OTHER WICCAN TOOLS

There are several other more minor, but still important tools that Wiccans use regularly.

Bells are an important Wiccan tool. As you start to read and learn about spells, don't be surprised to find that many include the ringing of a bell several times. Bells mark a transition in a ritual. A bell is often rung to begin and end a ritual, and may also be used throughout the ritual if the ritual has multiple steps.

Cauldrons are real, yes, and used by Wiccans in the Craft. They are probably the most well-known Wiccan tool, but there are many misconceptions about what they are used for. The optimal material for a cauldron is ceramic or cast iron, because they are intended to withstand large amounts of heat. Cauldrons can be filled with materials for a potion, for example, with a fire burning under the cauldron to warm and activate the ingredients. They can also be filled with small coals and used to burn herbs and incense.

Brooms are another commonly known Wiccan tool, but they aren't used for flight as seen in cartoons and movies. Wiccans use brooms to symbolically sweep away lingering energies. Because it is used for this ritual purpose, brooms are often handmade.

Finally, bowls are a simple and easily accessible tool for any Wiccan. Bowls are used to hold water (rainwater is best but any naturally occurring water may be used), salt, petals, herbs, or any number of other ingredients.

# CONCLUSION

After all this discussion of the tools of the Craft, it is important to remember as a beginner that absolutely none of these tools are a requirement. Wicca is about communing with nature. Communing with nature attunes your natural abilities.

If you don't have access to tools yet, take advantage of the natural world around you. Go outside, visit a park, go on a hike, admire the mountains and the sea, meditate over the flow of the rivers, absorb the light of the sun and the moon, take time to stargaze. There are plenty of ways to connect with your inner Wiccan without spending any money at all.

# CHAPTER 5: PRACTICING MAGIC

Once you feel in touch with nature and your inherent ability, it is wise to start learning about and practicing beginner magick. There's no need to rush into elaborate, confusing rituals with ingredients you've never heard of. With practice and patience, you will feel more in tune with your abilities. As you start to explore, you will eventually learn what elements of the Craft suit you best. Experimenting is important in early phases. The best way to learn is to read and to put your new knowledge into action.

This chapter focuses on two things. The first is education. Even if you're not ready for spells just yet, learning about them is the first step. Secondly, this chapter endeavors to teach you beginner's magick that is simple, effective, and harmless.

# MAGICK AND THE PHYSICAL WORLD

While Wiccans believe we all are born with inherent magickal talents, these talents are not absurd fictional miracles. There's no spell that will change the color of your eyes or make you taller, no spell that can create something from nothing. When learning about your talents and abilities, it is important to remember to be realistic. While some Wiccans have talents that are certainly spectacular, they operate within the laws of science.

Because of Wiccan reverence for nature, there is also Wiccan reverence for science. Wiccan beliefs do not contradict scientific findings. On the contrary, Wiccans are motivated to learn about science to deepen their understanding of the natural world, how it was formed, and most importantly how to preserve it.

Interestingly, scientific advancement has confirmed much that witches already knew. Witches of old had an intuitive understanding of the energy of all things, in addition to a wide range of knowledge regarding herbal medicine. Older scientific views perceived mind and matter to be separate completely (recall the phrase "mind over matter"). Witches have always known that mind and matter are one and the same, and of course science has confirmed that the mind functions because of the mechanisms of the brain, which is made of physical matter.

The brain is a powerful organ, and the power of thought is not to be underestimated. Thought-based practices, within Wicca but also in traditions like Buddhism that promote meditation and mindfulness, have been proven to cause actual positive change in our lives. Wiccans promote a focus on the positive, and cleansing of that which is negative. That is not to say that changing the way we think is a simple endeavor, however.

The Hermetic Principles or Hermetic Laws are a set of ancient laws that are important to Wiccan practice. We will not cover all of the seven principles here, because it is not obligatory to know them, especially for beginners, but we will touch on the most important ones and their basis in science.

An important Hermetic Principle is the Law of Attraction. This law simply states that positive thinking encourages positive outcomes. Part of the reason for this is because when we are in a positive state of mind, we are more likely to be aware and in control of our emotions and behaviors. Magick is of course much more complex than thinking positively, but regardless there is a sound psychological basis for this principle within modern scientific understandings of the brain and behavioral psychology.

The most emphasized Hermetic Principle in Wicca is called the Law of Correspondence. If you've ever heard the Wiccan phrase "as above, so below", this law is the basis for that saying. This means that whatever affects the macrocosm of the Universe in turn affects the microcosm, and vice versa. Some scientists refer to this as the Butterfly Effect. The Law of Correspondence also teaches us that time is only one dimension, in a Universe that experiences neither time nor space.

Because the Law of Correspondence teaches us that the Higher Planes and the Lower Planes are interconnected, intentions are very important when conducting magick practices. Whatever energy you put into the Universe may have a great effect, and may even be harmful to another, which is against the Wiccan rede.

Modern physics has discovered that at the atomic level, all material things are composed of matter and energy. This is compatible with the Hermetic Law of Vibration. All atoms vibrate and therefore constantly emit energy. Atoms vibrate at different frequencies, which creates the different states of matter (solids, liquids, and gases).

We perceive colors because of the phenomena of vibration. Light vibrates at different frequencies, which creates the spectrum of color. Witches can and do pick up on and use these different energies in their practice. By understanding the energy of the world around us, Wiccans tune into that energy and are able to connect it to their own personal energy. Wiccans can also use this energy conversely to communicate with the energy of the Universe.

Chakra therapy is based on this understanding of color (amongst other things). Aligning one's chakras is a way to rebalance one's energy to reap spiritual and physical benefits.

Because the physical world involves so many complex variables, it is impossible even for physicists and other scientists to accurately account for every unknown. The same is true for Wiccans. Spells and rituals may go awry due to forces that had not been accounted for.

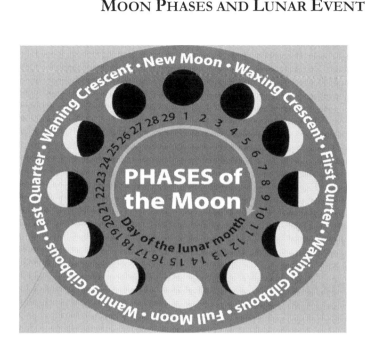

Whether or not you feel a significant connection to the moon, the phases of the moon have an effect on the magickal abilities of Wiccans. Different phases of the moon call for different phases of reflection. When the moon is full, the time is ripe for magick. It is best to keep a lunar calendar or use an app with reminders, to be aware of how the moon may be affecting you.

The cycles of the moon represent, for traditional Wiccans, the life cycle of women embodied by the Triple Goddess. The Triple Goddess in the form of the moon experiences birth at the new moon, and completion at the full moon. When the moon is waxing, or growing brighter, a Wiccan's power is growing stronger day by day. The waxing moon symbolizes the Goddess's journey from Maiden to Mother. When the moon is waning, or growing darker, it is time for Wiccans to rest, reflect, study, and prepare for the next lunar cycle. The waxing moon represents the Goddess's journey from Mother to Crone.

The new moon is a time to think about your goals for the coming month. It is a time of reflection rather than a time for action. The next moon phase, the waxing crescent moon, is a time to begin creating plans on how to achieve those goals. The first quarter moon is when Wiccans can begin to move towards these goals and think creatively. The waxing gibbous moon a time of significant power, where Wiccans feel in harmony with the forces of nature and prepare the rituals for the coming full moon.

During the full moon, there are many things that can be done. Crystals, water, and other magickal tools can be set out for cleansing and to charge with lunar energy. If you work with a group, consider having an esbat to celebrate, socialize, and practice together. If you are a solitary witch, the full moon is a perfect time to perform spells, enchant objects, or do any other important magickal work. Don't forget in all the hustle and bustle to stop and enjoy the beauty of this special evening!

During the waxing period of the moon, celebrate all you have achieved that month. Remember that every day you become wiser, even as the magick of the lunar cycle winds down. Let go of the past, and understand that mistakes are opportunities for growth. During the dark moon, remember that all things happen in their own time. Banishing spells are strongest during the dark moon, but take great care. The spell may be more powerful than you realize, and someone you could have reconciled with may disappear from your life permanently.

A lunar eclipse occurs when the the moon is completely covered by the shadow of the Earth. While logic may tell us this would make the moon appear dark, the moon actually turns a magnificent, ethereal red color. It is a reflection of a million sunrises. This is often referred to as a blood moon.

Some Wiccans believe that during a total lunar eclipse, the moon represents every part of its cycle at once. This is because in a single night you can watch the Earth's shadow turn the moon through every phase, a complete waxing and waning. This effect is useful for multi-part spells that might otherwise have to be spread out throughout a month.

About every two or three years there comes a month where the moon will be full twice. This second full moon is known as a blue moon. This is the origin of the phrase "once in a blue moon". That saying has significance to Wiccans. A blue moon is thought to be twice as powerful as a full moon, and therefore magick can be performed that could only happen once in a blue moon.

# CHAKRAS: BALANCING MIND, BODY, AND SPIRIT

Chakra is a sanskrit word meaning "wheel". Chakras are energy centers that are associated with an area of the body. Each chakra is associated with a color, and certain abilities and bodily functions. If your chakras are unbalanced, you may feel spiritually blocked. This happens even to experienced Wiccans. The trick is learning to identify the symptoms of imbalance. Chakras are also associated with physical and mental ailments, but aligning your chakras is not an adequate replacement for professional medical attention.

The concept of chakras comes from ancient Indian Hinduism, as well as Japanese, Chinese, and Tibetan Buddhism. The tradition was introduced to the West by renowned psychologist Carl Gustav Jung.

Chakra blockages can develop from trauma, negative experiences, unhealthy beliefs, insecurity, or self-doubt. The day-to-day stresses of life also gradually misalign the chakras. Chakra alignment can be done several ways, and is actually quite simple. It is an excellent way for a beginning Wiccan to get in touch with their mind, body, and spirit.

There are seven main chakras and signs of imbalance:

1. Root Chakra. An unaligned root chakra will cause you to have difficulties meeting your basic needs. The color of the root chakra is red, and it is located at the front of the body near the pelvis.

2. Sacral Chakra. Imbalance of this chakra manifests as confusion or difficulty with sexuality, and infertility. Its color is scarlet, and it is located in the lower abdomen near the stomach.

3. Solar Plexus Chakra. This chakra is linked to unhealthy eating habits, substance abuse, and depression. The color associated with it is yellow, and it is located above the belly button and below the sternum.

4. Heart Chakra. Signs of imbalance of the heart chakra include difficulty with love, relationships and compassion. Its color is gold, and its location is the center of the upper chest.

5.     Throat Chakra. The throat chakra is associated with your inner voice and your ability to communicate. Imbalance can cause anxiety, nightmares, and a fear of speaking your truth. Its color is blue-green, and it is located on the front base of the neck.

6.     Third Eye Chakra. Symptoms of imbalance with this chakra may cause a lack of inspiration, problems sleeping, and psychic misinterpretations. The color associated with the third eye chakra is indigo, and it is located above and between the eyes, on the forehead.

7.     Crown Chakra. The crown chakra is associated with inspiration and oneness with the cosmos. Imbalance may cause a loss of spiritual direction, headaches, confusion, and worry. Its color is violet, and it is located at the top of the head, slightly to the back,

The simplest way to align your chakras is through meditation. This is a visualization exercise, but it is important not only to "see" but to feel the energies as well. First, sit up straight and allow your shoulders to fall in a relaxed position. Relax and prepare with some deep breathing. Next, imagine whichever chakra you wish to balance as an orb. The orb should be the color of the chakra. Then, breathe deeply and imagine each breath fills the orb up until it is the size of a beach ball. Acknowledge and cope with any emotional pain you may find.

If meditation isn't your thing, each chakra can also be aligned by communing with nature or engaging in a meaningful activity that exercises that specific energy. Wearing the color of the chakra and/or eating foods associated with that chakra will also restore balance.

The root chakra can be aligned by taking care of your physical body. Remember to exercise and get adequate rest. Working in a garden or making art with clay such as pottery will also align this chakra. Red foods like beets and pomegranates can help, too.

In order to balance the sacral chakra, it is best to seek an encounter with natural water. This could mean swimming in a lake, ocean, or river. It could also mean walking in the rain or watching a storm. Oranges and carrots are good options to align this chakra.

Balancing the solar plexus chakra is done through education. Read a book, take a class, do a crossword puzzle. Sunshine can also balance this point of energy. Chamomile and lemon teas are useful as well.

The heart chakra is balanced by nature walks and quality time with family and friends. Nurture your relationships and express love. Ginger is a wonderful remedy for the heart chakra.

Your throat chakra can be balanced by singing, doing creative writing, and having important, deep conversations. Blueberries nourish the inner voice associated with the throat chakra.

The third eye chakra is most effectively balanced by taking time to go stargazing or walking in the light of the moon. Keeping a journal can also balance your third eye chakra. Associated foods are figs and black currants.

Finally, to balance the crown chakra, try getting in touch with your dreams. This means both the dreams you have while asleep and your goals in life. Keep a dream journal or make a vision board to regain your direction. Plums, lavender, and amethyst are useful in restoring balance to this center of inspiring energy.

Keeping your energies in balance will help you achieve harmony on the inside and the outside. If you've never balanced your chakras before, it is recommended to do so before you begin practicing Wicca. If your energies aren't in sync, your spirit won't be either, and you won't be able to properly focus your magickal senses.

# SPELLS

Spells are magickal rituals that require symbolism, specific materials, incantations, concentration, and faith. The purpose of spells is to channel energy to enact some kind of change in a situation. For example, an author experiencing writer's block may perform a spell for creativity.

Spells date back to ancient Egypt and the Zoroastrian Magi, who in turn influenced the practices of Roman and Greek pagans. Ancient Norse traditions also involved this sort of ritual magick.

Spells can be directed at the self or at another, and can be positive or negative. However, performing negative magick against someone else goes against the Wiccan rede to do no harm. In fact, it is unwise to cast any sort of spell on someone else without their informed consent. Positive spells are sometimes called "blessings", or more archaically "enchantments". Negative spells are known as "hexes" or "curses".

Spells follow a specific formula in order to achieve the desired magickal effect. While the formula is important, what is most important is your intention and focus. It is impossible to cast a spell you don't believe in. Remember to be patient as a beginner, because your abilities may not yet be honed enough to cast certain spells.

One important rule when doing any kind of magick but especially spells is to pull energy from sources around you. If you pull energy from only your own resources, you will often feel drained, lethargic, and sometimes even hungry. This is the reason spells typically involve tools, but energy can also be drawn from nature itself.

Regardless of what spell you choose to perform, there are steps you should take to prepare for the ritual beforehand. The first step is to prepare your body and your mind. It is recommended to bathe before performing a spell. Some witches anoint themselves with relevant oils. If you have a special attire you prefer to use to perform magick, make sure the clothes are clean. Take time to meditate to relax and focus the mind.

If you are working indoors the next step is to cleanse your workspace. This can be done using crystals, by sprinkling salt around the perimeter, or by smudging (burning white sage). Other options sprinkling rainwater or water purified by the full moon. Clear the clutter from the area in which you plan to work so there will be no interfering energies or distractions.

Now it's time to draw your circle. Not all Wiccan traditions do this, but it is the dominant tradition. The circle is meant to channel energy from the four cardinal directions. Water is represented by the North, Air by the East, Fire from the South, and Earth from the West. Creating a circle consecrates the space. You can trace the circle with your finger or a wand or athame, or you can physically draw one. Inside the circle, draw a pentagram. This circle is called a pentacle.

What happens after this varies from spell to spell. As a beginner, you can learn spells from reputable sources online (beware of phonies), but eventually you will have enough knowledge to begin writing your own spells.

Spells typically have an incantation, or a spoken verse that invokes your desires. It is common for these verses to rhyme. The incantation can invoke a deity, or even a planet or the moon for assistance. Incantations should be finished with the phrase "so mote it be".

Spells typically end by casting off a symbolic item. It could be burning a sigil (see next section), burning herbs, or something as simple as snuffing out a candle. Do keep in mind that you should never blow a candle out if possible. There are special devices made to snuff candles, but you can also use sand or water.

The final part of a spell is giving thanks. This could be an expression of gratitude to nature or any spirits or deities you invoked to aid you.

## SIGILS: THE CONDUITS OF INTENTION

Sigils are are symbols that represent an intention. Commonly used for protection, sigils require activation. Some sigils can be activated merely with focused intention. Other Wiccans prefer to burn copies of sigils to release their energy. Sigils are considered to be a basic, easy form of magic, perfect for beginners.

While you can easily find sigils for anything you could think of online, creating sigils is typically considered a very personal thing. Creating your own sigils is easier than you think, and can actually be fun and meditative.

When creating your sigil, make sure you are in a calm, quiet place with minimal distractions. Because sigils are manifested intentions, it is important that you completely focus on your intention during the process of creating or carving a sigil. If you become distracted, it is highly recommended that you start from the beginning.

To create your own sigil, you must first decide what your intention is. Your intention should be put into the form of a short, simple sentence. For example, "I am safe and calm". Once you have your sentence, depending on your tradition, the vowels may be removed from the sentences. From the remaining consonants, use each only a single time in your sigil. For the sentence used as an example, the consonants used would be "m, s, f, n, d, l".

The next step is your opportunity to get creative and truly connect with the sigil. Using the remaining consonants from your intention sentence, begin to create a shape by connecting and overlapping the letters. You can make the letters into simpler shapes like swirls, lines, and circles. When you feel you have created a shape that represents your intention, you are finished.

It's fine if you don't like your first try. It's common for witches to take their time drafting different versions until they are satisfied with the aesthetic of the sigil. By drawing your own sigil, the sigil contains elements of your personal energy and can be more effective.

You can carve sigils into candles and burn the candle to activate the energy of the sigil. Some Wiccans use sigils in cooking. For example, a kitchen witch may draw a sigil on the bottom of a pie crust to infuse the pie with protective energy and love. Another easy way is to draw a sigil in a cup using honey before pouring tea over it. Some witches draw sigils in their private notebooks to protect them from prying eyes.

# BATH MAGICK

Bath magick is a fun and easy way to begin performing rituals. It has the benefit of doubling as a form of self-care, which promotes self-worth and self-love. Loving the natural world includes loving oneself, as Wiccans believe we are united with nature. Cultivating a positive opinion of yourself will also increase your confidence in your abilities, and empower you to continue seeking knowledge and improving your Craft!

Different bath products have different magickal uses. The ingredients used are important, but there are very few if any bath products made with ingredients that would manifest a bad result. Either way, researching the components of your bath products is a great way to begin committing correspondences to memory. Handmade bath products are better than those produced by machines, but use whatever is available to you.

Bath salts can be used when you want to cleanse your spirit and your subconscious mind. Both salt and water have purifying qualities. Bathing with salts is an excellent way to prepare for a spell. Bubble baths are useful for when you want to be immersed in something in the conscious mind. Being surrounded by bubbles is symbolic of being submersed in your desires, thereby willing positive things into existence. This is sometimes called manifesting.

Bath bombs symbolically explode to push something rapidly into existence. Maybe you want to be kinder, or more spontaneous. This is a high-energy way to manifest your intentions. Bars of soap are great for carving sigils in. Thoroughly washing your body in the soap also covers you with your intentions, and the lingering scent will carry those intentions with you throughout the day.

You can also add flower petals into the bath as well as some teas. Fruity teas should be avoided because sugar can cause yeast infections, but chamomile is a relaxing, safe option. Rose petals in the bath will encourage love and romance. Lavender promotes calmness and peace of mind.

The faucet of the bath can represent flushing new, pure vibrations into your life. The drain of the bath is also symbolic. It can either represent flushing out negative energy, or represent sending your intentions out into the world.

You can enhance the ritual by playing music that complements your intentions, lighting candles, and by keeping crystals nearby. Many crystals will degrade if immersed in water, so this is not recommended.

# CONCLUSION

Whether or not you choose to observe the year and a day guideline, it is wise to have a period dedicated to learning the Craft before you begin your practice. This protects you and those around you from potential unintended effects of inexperienced magick. Only you know when you are truly ready to begin. Trust your instincts, but remember that it's not a race! Everything will come to you in your own time.

# CHAPTER 6: FINDING YOUR NICHE

With all this new information, it's easy to become overwhelmed. But choosing your path in Wicca is all about what traditions, rituals, and practices you connect with the most. Your Craft doesn't have to be like anyone else's, it can and in many ways should be completely unique to your spiritual needs and beliefs.

Some traditional Wiccans believe in the concept of "a year and a day". This is the idea that a beginning witch should devote a year and one day to only learning and studying the Craft. This is most common within covens that have an initiation process once this time period has passed. If you want to practice with a group, this learning period also gives you time to learn about and bond with the other Wiccans in your coven. It also provides time for a beginner to familiarize themselves with the rules and traditions of the group.

Some solitary witches value this tradition and follow it, but many Wiccans don't believe in an exact set period of time. Of course it is encouraged to learn about and understand the Craft before you practice, lest you make a mistake and cause yourself or someone else harm by accident. The learning period, however long it may be for you, is also a sign of respect for the Craft.

It shows that you know Wicca is not a fad or a phase, but something to be taken seriously.

# CHOOSING YOUR PATH

Outside of the major traditions, there are still many different acknowledged "types" of witches. Most witches fall into more than one category. By learning about each path, you can start to see what might interest you, and do further research on that subject to begin to specialize your knowledge. Don't be afraid to change your mind, and don't be afraid to experiment, as long as you do no harm.

*Eclectic witches* are Wiccans who combine many different beliefs, ideas, and traditions into their practice. An eclectic witch may worship multiple pantheons. Eclectic witches value practices from all cultures. They may practice divination from different areas of the world. Eclectic witches are almost always solitary, meaning they don't work with a group though they may participate in community gatherings for festivals.

*Green witches*, also known as garden witches or forest witches, are attracted to all things green. Green witches practice most of their magick outdoors. Many keep personal gardens, or grow houseplants if a garden is not available to them. They have a deep love for plants, flowers, herbs, and trees. Green witches are able to sense and connect with the spirits of plants, and prefer to use home-grown items for their Craft. Some even make offerings to their plants, or place crystals in the soil if the plant is potted.

Green witches are herbalists who have a wide range of knowledge about their local flora. They can identify plants by sight. They also gain a large range of knowledge about medicinal and poisonous plants through their diligent, passionate studies.

A *hedge witch* is a Wiccan who is skilled with spirit work. These individuals cross the metaphorical hedge to the other side for answers and guidance. Hedge witch is the modern word for a shaman. Many witches prefer to avoid identifying as shamans unless they descend from a shamanistic culture, because it can be appropriative and disrespectful to claim another culture's title.

Hedge witches communicate with spirits in a variety of ways. This is called hedgecrossing, no matter what method is used. Some meet and speak with spirits through lucid dreams. Lucid dreaming often comes naturally to a hedge witch, but it is a skill most can learn. Astral projection and and trances are other ways to communicate with the spirit world.

*Kitchen witches* reject a lot of traditional perspectives, and strongly believe in finding magick in the mundane. These individuals thrive while cooking, making teas, brews, and working with herb and spice blends to enchant meals and drinks. If these tasks need to be performed either way, why not make them magickal?

Kitchen witches imbue their cooking with medicinal and magickal properties. For example, one might season food with rosemary to provide protection for the family and friends who will consume the food. Kitchen witches often have collections of recipes passed down from many generations.

An *augury witch* is a Wiccan who is able to interpret natural omens. Aurugy is an ancient Roman tradition. Augury witches often work with travelers to help guide them along the correct path. Augurs may interpret weather patterns or the appearance of sacred animals such as birds.

*Hereditary witches* are those who have other witches in the family. Some hereditary witches come from a long line of Wiccans. Others may find out they have a connection to Wicca by learning of an ancestor who practiced and forming an interest in reclaiming the Craft.

You do not have to choose any label for your practice. Labels are meaningful and helpful to some, but can be confining and smothering for others. Some witches feel connected to the stars, some to fire, some to the ocean and some to the mountains. Commune with nature and the answers will come from within you.

## COMMUNITY OUTREACH

Whether you're a solo witch or part of a coven, community is an important part of Wicca. Beginner witches are often affectionately known as "baby witches" and are cherished by the Wiccan community. Every Wiccan remembers the beginning of their journey and the kindness they received from others following the Old Religion. You will find they are eager to pay it forward by offering tips, friendship, and sometimes even mentorship.

Only about 1% of the world practices Wicca, which can make it challenging to find others in your area. Another obstacle is the stigma that still surrounds Wiccan beliefs. Many people don't understand the difference between white and black magick. They fear Wiccans as devil-worshippers who summon demons to do their bidding. However, as you know by this point, that couldn't be farther from the truth. Regardless, many Wiccans remain silent about their beliefs to avoid judgment from their friends, families, and communities.

The best way to connect with other Wiccans is online. Try searching social media tags for groups dedicated to the Craft. Be wary of those who would take advantage of you, and take the same precautions you normally would when communicating with strangers on the internet.

Luckily, the vast majority of the Wiccan community is warm and welcoming. Reaching out to other Wiccans is one of the best ways to find reliable information about the Old Religion. They can provide book recommendations written by qualified occult authors that provide legitimate information. When searching for information about Wicca on the internet, keep your wits about you; there is no shortage of phonies publishing misleading and incorrect information.

# CONCLUSION

If you haven't realized it by now, Wicca can be full of contradictions. While this might be confusing for beginners, it is part of the beauty of the religion. As you continue to read and learn about Wicca, you will continue to encounter these contradictions. Your favorite authors might have different methods of casting a circle, or you may hear fellow Wiccans disputing the origins of certain traditions. When you come to these crossroads, it is time to tune into your intuition and make whatever decision makes most sense for you.

But you don't have to make these decisions all at once. In fact, it's always better to wait until you have adequate information before choosing any path. Research really is the name of the game when it comes to understanding ancient practices.

There is room for everyone who feels called to the Craft, and that means there is room for you, too!

# ASTROLOGY UNCOVERED:

# INTRODUCTION TO ASTROLOGY

Twenty degrees up and down from the ecliptic and celestial equator, 12-star groups can be found and the name "Zodiac" was given to them in the dawn of times. This name allegedly comes from the Greek term "zodion", which means the "animal belt", and almost all of the names in it refer to animals. A common belief is that the names of the star constellations and their groupings came from the first hunters and nomads because they needed a proven method for orientation. When the age of agriculture arrived, determining the seasons of the year became necessary, and the motion of the Sun and Moon through heavenly constellations became determining factors for the meteorological and even political successes or failures.

Archeology has found firm evidence that the early humans from prehistoric times had an understanding of celestial movements and events. Many discoveries show that people of those ages carefully watched the sky and that they had precise calendars. Those calendars mainly portrayed the motion of the Moon, the Sun, and oddly, Venus and the star system of Pleiades. Why prehistoric men would have such an interest in aligning with the Pleiades or even Venus, no one knows, but this also raises another question. Why would prehistoric people even want to follow and measure the motion of celestial bodies to the extent that they were building huge systems of stones, and later on temples, to be able to track the Sun or other significant heavenly objects? Was it just for orientation, which is useful for hunting? Certainly not.

Astrology, together with astronomy because they were considered as one science, originated in Babylonia and Sumer. Both are considered one of the oldest natural science in the world. How come that the cradle of civilization had such knowledgeable astronomers/astrologers? If we forget about the official history for a moment and start speculating, could aliens, known as Annunakis, have taught them this art?

Scriptures mention that "angels" taught humankind the art of metallurgy, medical treatments and remedies. They even advised women how to start applying makeup and of course, they showed us how to "read the sky".

The whole area of Mesopotamia, including Babylonia, Sumer, and Assyria, is rich in archeological artifacts related to astronomical/astrological themes and many of them are dated older than 2000 BC. Babylonian priests were known for their superior knowledge about planets, stars, eclipses, and all geometrical aspects those bodies can form, which was used mainly for political predictions. Bear in mind that in those ages, there were no daily horoscopes published for the common people. Natal horoscopes were drawn just for the members of the royal families and astrology was also very useful for selecting the proper dates for building new cities or attacking enemies. This remained the norm almost until the last century because the natal charts of the "common people" were seen as absolutely unimportant.

Enuma Anu Enlil is the most famous archaeological artifact from these times. It is the compilation of 70 cuneiform tablets, which describe 7000 astronomical/astrological omens. During the following thousands of years, the science of mathematics was also developed, which was used for very precise calculations of the celestial positions and the creation of the first ephemerides. From Babylonian times, humankind inherited the habit of naming the planets after the gods and to associate them with mythical stories.

To this day, many modern astrologers claim that the original and most precise astrology called "Eden Astrology" can still be found in the areas of Iraq and Iran, but it is extremely hard to find astrologers who are practicing this art and who are willing to teach it, because astrology is outlawed in those two countries. Myth or truth, it's still hard to discover the answer.

Astrology was brought to Egypt around the 5th century BC by the Persians. However, Egypt was an extremely developed country in those times and it's hard to believe that they didn't know about planets and stars until the Persians came to conquer them. Whatever the case may be, Alexander the Great founded Alexandria and by the second century BC, this town became the location of the most famous university in the world. Ptolemy wrote an extensive work, *Tetrabiblos*, about the planetary characteristics, exaltations, triplicities, and many other basic facts. In those moments astrology, as we know it today, was born. Horoscope charts were made and analyzed in a very similar way as they are done today.

The knowledge about the stars was widely spread across the Greek territories and it was recognized as Chaldean (Babylonian) art. It continued to spread, naturally, over the whole Roman Empire and when the great kingdom fell, knowledge about astrology remained a secret

While the dark ages held power over Europe, the world of Islam continued the tradition of Alexandria's Great school. Many scholars went east, running away from rising the Christian dogma against natural sciences. The city of Baghdad became the new center of knowledge and many sciences in the forms as we know them today were founded there. The Arab world researched methodically so-called "fixed" stars and their influence on the life of our planet, and classified the system of calculating mutual relations between celestial bodies, which is known today as "Arabic parts".

When we look at the east, we are amazed by the levels of knowledge Indian or Hindu astrology achieved. The first notion of this art can be found in Vedas, which claimed to be the oldest known texts. By the times of Alexandria's greatest breakthroughs, Vedic astrologers had to deal with higher mathematics and very serious and precise astronomical observations. The legend goes that the ancient sage Bhrigu, one of the Saptarishis (seven sages who helped to create the universe), has all the horoscope charts of all people who were born and will be born on this planet.

Due to its close relation with astronomy Vedic or Hindu astrology deals with sidereal positions of planets and uses somewhat different types of aspects, while the meaning of all celestial bodies, zodiac signs and houses are the same as they are in the "western" school of astrology.

Chinese tradition is known for its concepts of yin and yang, and it uses somewhat different types of calculations, but astrology is present there from the ancient times and besides the popular Feng Shui, which deals with the energies of the Earth, Ba Zi art deals with heavens.

Over the Atlantic Ocean, Olmec and the Aztecs were known for their calendars and precise mathematical calculations when it comes to the position of our planets, especially Venus and, as you can guess, a constellation of Pleiades. However, later on, the Mayan calendar became the most recognized and famous calendar in the world.

Back in Europe, it didn't take a long time for astrology together with astronomy to rise again. Until seventeenth century, science was necessary if you wanted to become a doctor, for instance. All diagnostics and healing treatments were done according to the planets and stars. A Christian church wasn't so satisfied with this fact, but it was powerless due to the popularity and the cautious approach of astrologers in those ages.

However, when the era of humanism and education came, astrology was pronounced the occult science, or better yet, something which is not science at all. From that moment in time, it was separated from astronomy. An interesting fact is that Isaac Newton, the father of modern scientific thought, was the one to passionately love and study astrology.

A few hundred years have passed and astrology is back again. With the rise of modern psychology, astrology took a somewhat different turn, interpreting the planetary aspects through the inner or emotional states of human beings. Luckily, after decades of vague readings, astrology returned to its roots again, and as such, interprets the outer events and envisions the future.

Mistakes happen, indeed, but if the astrologer during the reading can see around 75-80% accurately your past, present and future events, challenges, losses, and triumphs, then you have found a quality consultant and you can count on that person to be your greatest ally for the planning of your future. Let's just not forget the words of JP Morgan: "Millionaires don't need astrologers, but billionaires do".

With this in mind and if you are interested in learning something more about yourself, you will find this book extremely useful, because it will help you to see clearly what are the meanings of the planets, signs, and houses in the horoscope chart and how to recognize your character, future challenges and even how to use those challenges for your success. This can be applied to all people and the most important part is that you will be able to predict the outcome of your relationships with others. You will also learn something about myths related to ancient gods and perhaps even have a little fun.

# *PLANETS*

Through the eyes of astrology, our lives are determined by celestial bodies; such as, fixed stars, meteor showers, various flying objects and so on, but to be able to read astrological charts, you have to learn the basic traits of the main heavenly "influencers" and these are: Sun, Moon, Mercury, Venus, Mars, Jupiter, Saturn, Uranus, Neptune and Pluto, as well as the North and South Nodes of the Moon - Rahu and Ketu.

## SUN

The ultimate deity in our little piece of this cosmos is the Sun. The Sun is the father of everything, the central body around which all others revolve. Its shine is the essence, the light, the life in us, and the energy source for photosynthesis, which is the basic metabolic process for plants and even for animals. We are all eukaryotes after all. Without the Sun, we are not able to exist. This is also the first god in any early religion and the founder of the yearly calendar because we have the spring and autumnal equinoxes, and the summer and winter solstices. Around those four points in time, all of our rituals were created and worshiped throughout the existence of humankind. Nothing else is so powerful and nothing else can create or destroy us like the Sun.

Its qualities are: center, masculine, warm and dry, royalty, generosity, responsibility, light, warmth, vitality, power, honor, glory, reputation, authority, healthy ego, stability, maturity, calm enthusiasm, goodness. If it's placed in an unfavorable position and in tense aspects with other planets, or points on the chart, it can result in: vanity, arrogance, narcissism, snobbism and so on.

The Sun, forming a beneficial aspect with the other planets, will always give the characteristics of someone who doesn't know about mean behavior, a person with classy manners, with good judgment, and a natural born leader. Its negative planetary aspects will portray a person who is pretentious, egoist, or untrustworthy; someone who ruins order or life itself.

The Sun is the king, a middle-aged man, rich, or in other terms, a very successful man. This star also represents the day of Sunday, the lion, cats in general, bees, royal and golden colors, castles, decorations, gold, glitter, expensive jewelry, blond hair in females, a man who loses his hair when it comes to males, France and all royal families. It is the vision and therefore symbolized with eyes. In male charts, it is mainly the right eye, in female charts – the left one. In the terms of medical astrology, the Sun is the heart, the spine and the bone marrow, vitamin D, and many claim that it is also vitamin A; all crucially important parts of body.

In the terms of music, according to Pythagorean ideas, this is the sound "do".

The conjunction of the Sun and Moon, and their placement close to the North or the South Nodes of the Moon and some fixed stars like the Pleiades, Hyades or Praesepe can show blindness. Positive aspects with the Moon bring unity between the will and emotions, and good relationships between parents. Negative aspects show the internal war between the masculine and feminine, between the father and mother in us, and metabolic turmoil.

If Mercury, or any other planet, is placed too close with the Sun, then it is considered as burnt, so in this case, reasoning is damaged by ego. In the other case, when Mercury is positioned a bit further, this describes a person with great intelligence and someone prone to leadership. Venus with the Sun in positive aspects will show an admirer of beauty and good manners. However, the opposite will indicate problems between emotions and pleasure on one, and ego pretensions on the other side. Mars and the Sun together in positive combinations will show courage and power, but in the negative terms, this is someone prone to conflicts and agitation.

The Sun and Jupiter point to the greatest ruler, the most spiritual teacher, genuine guru, but on the negative side this is someone who is gaining weight too fast, and someone who fights authority, creates obstacles, squanders money or other resources, and leads a shameful life. With Saturn, the Sun can represent a reputation earned by hard work and dedication, gains of properties and knowledge. In negative terms, this is the curse of the ancestors, the mark of trouble, of problems with the father or a fatherly figure, and a heavy burden to carry throughout the whole life.

Uranus and the Sun can form unusual psychology in a person and depending on the aspects, this can be a genius when it comes to scientific or technological breakthroughs, but it can also be someone with bipolar disorder or the plain "slave of fashion trends". With Neptune, the Sun gives the gift of art, especially poetry, knowledge of chemistry and biology, but the negative side can be shown as an inclination toward illusions of all sorts. With Pluto, this is the spirit with demonic powers which can create the highest good, as well as the lowest of the low.

# MOON

Lady Luna is the mother. Yes, the Earth is our real mother, but when it comes to the projection of celestial bodies someone had to take the role of the mother and having in mind that the Moon depends on the Sun reflecting its light on us during the night, Lady Luna is perceived as the dark side of the light in us. This is not necessarily bad, but opposite to order and masculine rules.

The motion of the Moon had been the basis of counting days, or nights, and creating "months" known as the lunar calendar. The Moon needs around 28 days to complete its circle and this is the center point of the small cycle in us in comparison to the "big" cycle based on the motion of the Sun.

Its qualities are: cold and moist, reflects the light, feminine, distanced, moody, responsive toward outer stimulation, psyche, strong fantasy, dependence, softness, wonderings, changes, suggestible, subjective. And all of these traits could become positive, negative or even both at the same time.

The Moon is the day of Monday, the mother in general, mother holding a baby, baby, people in general, like a nation, women, middle-aged women, sea, water, lake, night, coldness, water retention, water overflow. The Moon represents everything soft and with big eyes, fish and water creatures, wolves, dogs, slimy insects, blue, silver and even white colors, pearls, isolated places, mirrors, Holland and USA too, lighter and softer hair and skin, left eye in the male chart, right eye in the female chart.

In medical terms, the Moon rules the stomach, breasts, and womb, and when the woman is pregnant, the "full womb". It regulates the flow of water in our bodies and the lymph system. Together with Venus, this is mother's milk in female charts and it's the quality of sperm in male charts. It can be any of the vitamins coming from the B complex and in music, it's traditionally considered to be the note "Fa".

Too close to the Sun or in square or opposition with it, the Moon is dried out. Emotions have been burnt for the sake of the ego, survival or due to bad psychological "inheritance" coming from parents or parental figures. The good aspects are softening the will and advancing in life in accordance with feelings, not just logic.

Mercury and the Moon are two very odd friends if they make mutual aspects. In opposition or square, those two celestial bodies imply the liar or the cheater, or deceiver. If this is not the case, the person's feelings and thoughts are harmonized and well guided. Good aspects with Venus lead to delicate and elegant tastes, enjoyment in romance and food, while the opposite brings some sort of "soap opera" in the native's life because emotions and sense of pleasure differ. So when I know that I shouldn't eat that cake or I shouldn't seduce that married man but I can't resist, then the whole drama is born and this can lead to some spectacular resolutions. Looking on this from the brighter side, this is how literature was born and is created today…and how it will continue to be created.

The Moon and Mars are very special when coupled. Negatively speaking, Mars destroys the Moon, people become senseless, especially women, cruel and extremely aggressive in some cases. It can also show pain, injuries, and surgical interventions. On the positive side, Mars can give the Moon persistence and tenacity to go through most difficult tests in life. Jupiter is all about gaining weight with the Moon, water plus fat, but it can also describe the purity of the mind and the soul.

Saturn and the Moon are performing great when positioned in auspicious types of aspects. Discipline is above feelings and the person is ready to suffer or to reshape its soul and body to achieve success. Negatively, this is loneliness, long, chronic diseases, troubles with older feminine figures in life, especially mother or grandmother. With Uranus, it can point toward magnificent and extraordinary ideas or plain madness. Although the aspects with Neptune can look similar, in this case, the person can be an exquisite chemist, doctor, poet or saint, or on the other side, the dark side of the Moon, the person can be a drug addict, someone lost in the world of inner illusions and a skilled cheater.

Pluto and the Moon? Resurrection, the hardest tests for the body, the edge of losing the soul, "I just came from hell" type of thinking, type of smile, type of revenge.

# MERCURY

The mind, logic, logistics, operative memory, trickster, Jack of all trade and master of none, "trust me, I'm an engineer" type of showing off. "He" can "she" and "she" can return to "he" or the ultimate "it". Mercury is known as the messenger of the gods and it goes wherever no god or no man would even step. He or she is cold and dry and never further than 27 degrees from the Sun, which implies that logic is never apart from ego.

It represents communication, trading, short travel, marketing, streets, neighborhoods, hallways, markets, schools, offices, journalism, rumors, gossips, often "right to the point" references and information, healing, health and herbalism, nutrition, wheat, grass, seeds, nuts, vitamin C, small intestine, lungs, brain, nervous system, birds, insects in general, small animals; you can find Mercury everywhere. Wednesday is his day. In music, this is the tone "Mi" and in education, this is something you can apply in real life right now, a simple calculation, but very useful every time. The color orange, but it can change from honey to chestnut shades, also all pastel colors and shades of autumn leaves and fruits. From Belgium to Tunisia, from Brazil to Greece, you'll find him in many countries as the main ruler.

Mercury in good aspect with Venus is the skilled lover, sweet talker, and smooth operator. In approaching square or in a negative type of conjunction this couple points clearly toward a cheater or someone very unreliable, especially in a committed love relationship. This can also be the sign of rude or insolent language or even person's inner desires can look like this. With Mars, Mercury can lead someone toward enormous success in engineering professions, due to their mutual "fast thinker and skilled worker" symbiosis. In negative aspects, this is the sign of a very rude person, passive-aggressive, someone who had been beaten as a child and now beats others, problems with hands, palms, lungs, intestines.

Jupiter and Mercury's combination is the match made in heaven when paired properly by astrological aspects. Jupiter directs the soul toward the greatest heights of human achievements, purity of intentions and spirituality, while Mercury organizes the mind to be disciplined and fast when it comes to implementation of the noble Jupiter's teachings. The other way around is called total chaos of the mind. If you don't know exactly what this means, try to imagine an attempt to trade with God during meditation, and then try walking down the street with your eyes closed and your thoughts directed toward heavens. Some people can live like this, but not for too long, if someone else is not taking care of them all the time.

Saturn and Mercury together in the auspicious positions is the sign of a great mathematician, respectable and stable thinking and well spoken, especially as this person gets older. On the negative side, this is a problem with the speech or tongue, fear of speaking and expressing, loneliness when it comes to ideas and self-promotion and mind blocks.

Mercury and Uranus are known as the main trait of electricians, astrologers, geniuses and mad people. This is the basic model for electricity, in mind, in a body, in ideas. The conjunction of those two fast and furious celestial bodies frequently implies autoimmune diseases or neurological problems, or most likely both. In good aspects, this is the image of a spotless mind, but when bad times activate bad aspects of them, this is the clear danger of electrical stroke whether it comes from inside or outside sources. In those particular cases some medical diagnostic tools, like ultrasound or X-rays exams can damage such native.

A quality tarot card reader is known as someone with trines or sextiles between Neptune and Mercury. The same goes for a guitar player and if you add Venus to this formula, then you get the perfect musician, no matter what instrument is involved. Neptune is here to inspire, while Mercury serves to channel the message of intuition. If aspects between them are tense, this is the sign of a liar, cheater, or at least, messy speaker. Pluto and Mercury are indicating someone with heightened drama in communication or during usual daily obligations. This can also be the poisonous speech, but if positive, the person with this aspect can heal with just loud praying.

# VENUS

She is pleasure itself. Is this good? Not necessarily, because Venus has the longstanding reputation of someone who challenged the almighty God or the Supreme Power or Energy (choose whatever you like the best) and was punished for her ideas and deeds. In western astrology, Venus is considered as a female planet, but traditional views look at "her" like Lucifer, the light bearer, someone who was most beautiful, skilled and intelligent among all angels. Those characteristics slowly, but surely led him to believe that he can be better than the God (Sun) itself and in the end, he was punished by being expelled to the underworld. Vedic myth concerning Venus differ somewhat, but the conclusion is the same. You will be punished if you start imagining your greatness greater than the Supreme Greatness. Vanity can be hell sometimes.

Venus is beauty, harmony, elegance, desire for material security, dancing school, wardrobe, court of law, garden, flowers, jewelry, shiny stones, fashion, sweets, especially chocolates, perfumes, assessors, romance, romantic literature, poetry, music, dancing, sheep, all small and soft animals. She is cold and moist by nature and her colors are blue, green, turquoise and even white. Her day is Friday. Her lands are Austria, Switzerland, Canada, China, Argentina and most of all, she loves beauty through an order.

Her organs are the throat, lower jaw, thyroid gland, neck, skin, and kidneys. She regulates the blood pressure and the levels of copper in blood. And her favorite sports, besides noble types of joy, like ballroom dancing, are qigong or yoga, disciplines known for their power of balancing and harmonizing inner energies. She is the queen of vitamin E, something necessary for the beauty of the skin.

Venus is "La", of course.

With Mars, this is the basic story of love, romantic pursuing and carnal passion. Negative aspects between them can cause havoc in a person's life, but on the brighter side, this is how art was founded in the first place. Jupiter and Venus are true love and devotion for spiritual teachings and, also, true love and devotion toward a good and useful sugar daddy, while on the negative side this is the sign that the person is not capable to budget for expenses or expenses tend to build up no matter what other safety actions are previously taken.

Saturn and Venus mean stability and tradition if positioned fine. However, on the other side, this is life without love, without true love, frustration, and coldness. Great for sculptors, horrible for lovers. Uranus and Venus usually meet through social media, airplanes or any other unusual place and time. There is the spark, there is the fire and there is one big nothing after. Disappointment usually lasts the longest, but the mistakes tend to be repeated in the case that the person has negative aspects between those two planets. In a positive way, this is the sign of exclusive taste, unusual, but lasting love with the pilot, astronaut, and scientist and so on.

Astonishing, gorgeous, wonderfully magical can be the voice of Venus when joined with Neptune. This is the fairy, the angel, the purest of the pure, the softest of the soft and the sweetest of all sweet things in this realm. But, when those two are in the tense aspects, this is the cheater of all cheaters, carrier of venereal diseases, or it can be shown as various missionaries trying to buy your soul using all sorts of manipulative psychological techniques. And this is, also, passion toward alcohol and frequently illegal substances. Venus and

Pluto is the story of the Lord of the Underworld and his bride. Being positive or negative, this type of aspect always reminds us that there is a price we have to pay. The greater the pleasure – the greater the price will be.

# MARS

He is our drive for life, for sex, for action. He is a warrior in every one of us. Masculine, his nature is hot and dry, his color is red, naturally and he is all about breakthroughs, "cut and enter" philosophies, so he can also be an expert when it comes to surgery. Of course, he is courageous, open, truthful and direct. He loves to reside in fighting places like dojos and open grounds too. Swords, guns, machines, advancing through deserts, through jungles, through mountains, there is always a war going on, and something and someone has to be conquered. Mars is the enemy to every other planet, except Venus. Her softness and femininity are his final defeat, but he can't resist her and he won't be able to resist her until the time runs out in this universe.

When negatively positioned or aspected with other celestial bodies, he is so hard to handle, heavy when it comes to polemics; annoying, destructive, full of injuries, verbal or physical fights with no particular reason or outcome, psychopath, murderer, dog or war; he can be everything.

His sound is "So", his vitamin K. He rules Tuesday, and in the terms of medical astrology he is the nose, the muscles, genitals, blood, and controls the levels of iron or red blood cells directly. His animals are all aggressive animals, no matter how small or big they are, especially males in animal species. Countries under his heavenly government are Germany, Japan, Israel, Syria, and Korea.

With Jupiter, he can become a warrior priest, military doctor, dignified expert, but when their aspects are negative this is the sign of agitator, manipulator, spitfire type of guy, always in conflicts with authorities, but it can be also beneficial for entrepreneurs if they manage to get "the rules of the game". His association with Saturn brings exceptional strength and discipline, gaining the fortune in the second part of life and longevity. However, if positioned in negative aspects, this is traditionally considered to be the hardest planetary aspect there is in the whole science of astrology. World wars are starting with this seal in heavens, and personal lives are filled with such hard challenges which can extend beyond human imagination. Car accidents, permanent disabilities, killing someone out of duty, accidentally killing someone, tough decisions, ruined happiness for the rest of a person's life.

Mars and Uranus bring a dash of gunpowder, electricity followed with an explosion. Great for engineering, technical breakthroughs, thinking out of the box, sudden turnarounds, but for a better solution. Negatively positioned, those two planets indicate strongly the danger of car accidents, electric shock, sudden attack, sexual deviations and aggression, criminal mind and similar fast and furious events and people. Neptune can bring magnificent insights regarding sailing, astrophysics, higher mathematics, hydraulics, and pneumatics. This aspect also gives great intuition when it comes to taking action and not taking action, proper place, and proper moment to strike or to pull back. Their negative traits bring the worst out of the person. This is the cheater, deceiver, criminal type of guy ready to do anything low to get what he needs. It also indicates alcoholic psyche, substances abuse, no matter whether those substances are legal or illegal.

Pluto and Mars fall under the special category because the position of Pluto has to be prominently placed in the chart to be active. But this is all about highest drama there is, childhood trauma which can't be healed followed by great inner transformation. Good aspects indicate enormous strength, the power to bare an unbearable, explosive, but creative mind. While the bad aspect shows sudden danger, sudden death, sudden victory.

# JUPITER

This planet is a world of its own. Jupiter is almost like a little Sun in our system, with twelve satellites and the power to protect us from the outer cosmic bodies. He is all about expansion, education, broader views, religious teachings, long distance traveling, sailing over the open seas, archery, hunting, honor, noble tradition, synthesis of knowledge, law, and order, goodness, generosity. His day is Thursday, he is hot and moist and his color is bright yellow, but it can also be a bit darker, like saffron. Remember Buddhists or Hindi priests in their yellow or orange robes? This is the symbol for Jupiter.

In the terms of medical astrology, Jupiter is fat tissue and brain together with Mercury, liver and gallbladder, thighs, and buttocks, vitamin R. His animal is a horse or an elephant, but wild and free animals like deer or eagles all fall into his kingdom. It also loves to reside in woods and open spaces. His lands are

Australia, Chile, South Africa, North Africa, Portugal, Scandinavia. According to Pythagoras's teachings, his sound is "Ti".

Of course, there are negative traits related to this planet; this is the main rule of the life itself. Jupiter can also gain weight fast, he can become overwhelming, endlessly unrestrained, vain, boring, manipulative and with a dirty mind or emotions. People often blame Saturn for their obstacles, and especially health problems. But at the same time, they tend to forget that no other planet can strike you so hard and fast with such expansion as Jupiter can do it.

In association with Saturn, this planet gives an exceptional and structured type of thinking and planning, achieving properties and wealth in general terms. These are constructive and systematic methods in business, agriculture, governmental tasks and in education. Those types of positive aspects are extremely significant in personal horoscopes, and astrologers in general tend to assume that all founders of main religions, like Buddha, Jesus, and Mohammed, had this aspect prominent in their natal charts. Negatively placed, energy exchanged between Saturn and Jupiter can lead to the loss of position or reputation, troubles with court cases and law, tendency for self-destruction, persecution, and serious problems for the father or grandfather of the person.

When you think about lottery gains, you have to associate Jupiter with Uranus in the heavenly formula for sudden success. This is also the image of the eccentric mind, unconventional thoughts, and often people's heroes during the times of war, and in some cases genius. Negative traits of this aspect are indicating a crazy person, someone who squanders his talent for worthless inventions, sudden losses, aggressive atheism, great problems caused by educated people.

Jupiter with Neptune is all about spirituality and the highest moral standards one person can acquire through life. This is the symbol for the accomplished saint who became the true role model for the masses, the teacher, and the avatar. A person with this aspect is not capable of distinguishing others related to their social levels, castes, races. The same person is deeply emotionally involved with suffering and resolving all problems regarding the suffering of people, animals, plants, the Earth itself. The negative side of this aspect can also show its grandiose or the wideness of evil because the person can become involved in a cult. This is the clear sign of someone who is the member or the leader of the religious sect, but political parties can be in play here also. Manipulation and humiliating perpetration, very twisted and often sick crimes are all present with this aspect.

Pluto with Jupiter can show the depthless quality of the mind. So-called "zeroing" when understanding is at its highest level that it negates itself. Singularity of spiritual thoughts, fast and strong transformation, resurrection, transmutation. Negative aspects between those two planets indicate horrible suffering due to religious beliefs, egoism and ecstasy, triumph through total destruction, victory through loss and vice versa.


# SATURN


This is probably the most feared planet in the whole Solar system. It's known as the "Ring Pass Not" because planet Saturn with its recognizable rings was considered to be the border guardian of our sky and on the other side the mystery of the spiritual realm begins.

This celestial body is directly related to the flow of time, discipline, persistence, durability, seriousness, responsibility, reasoning, but it also governs properties, stones, especially precious pieces, old castles, graveyards, crypts, basements, top of the mountains, hard terrains in general, goats, hogs, mice, all small, but strong animals are his favorite pets, because they never give up.

Bulgaria, Tibet, India, Russia, Ethiopia, Iran, these are the countries marked by Saturn. His nature is cold and dry and it rules during the Saturdays. Prominent colors are black, of course, ashy shades, even purple or ultraviolet in rare cases. In the terms of medical part of astrology, this planet represents the bones, teeth and knees, skeletal system and our ability to stand upright. And it is also vitamin D, crucially important for the health of the bones. His sound is "Re" and he is portrayed as the old skinny man with prominent nose and ears.

The negative side of Saturn is a life full of obstacles, hunger, poverty, chronic diseases, deadly illnesses, freezing cold, endless waiting for things to get better, lack of resources, lack of love, lack of everything. The extreme pressure which can break or destroy many, but from exceptional ones Saturn makes exquisite jewels. Its symbol is the diamond because this is just the piece of coal which had to go through enormous pressures and temperature changes to become the hardest one and the most beautiful, most precious clear stone.

Together with Uranus, Saturn tends to preach about the ideas of socialism, communism, revolutions, how poor and insignificant rise against rich and royals to establish the new kingdom of equality. This usually happens through blood and new types of oppression. This can also indicate new ideas regarding science with results acquired through long and laborious research work. The negative side shows a longing for authority with unclear causes or outcomes, drastic behavior, damaged neurology and psyche, anarchism, eccentricity, problems with authorities or with the law.

Neptune and Saturn are good companions when it comes to the oil and gas industry, all things related to mining, especially underwater drilling, and excavations. This is also the sign of someone who can perceive the geometry of space or spaces together in the mind or in the speculative realms of geometry. Good for "serious" types of music, old instruments, legends, myths and ancestral teachings. It can lead some people to become the channel between the world of the dead and the world of the living. Negatively this aspect describes the liar, someone who doesn't just lie but twists the truth, especially in the political sense. Manipulation over masses through news or education, strange diseases, epidemics, death by stifling, nicotine or any other source of smoking addiction, asthma, cataracts.

Saturn and Pluto are considered to be the sign of an ancestral curse, black magic, dead bodies, massive destruction, investigation, archeology, forensics, sadism, ascetics. There are really no just good or just bad aspects between those two planets. Everything related to them is truly related to the greatest depths of our beings, the essence of the soul, reaching for the demon and dancing with him.

And this is the moment when we have exited the traditional heavens and discovered the new planets. Their influence wasn't so prominent before their discoveries, but from the point in time when we became aware of them, they incorporated into our lives and took the meanings and symbolism of our inventions too.

Planets outside the traditional astrology are mainly considered as the indicators of collective and social trends. They are more important for the political, cultural or technological changes than personal ones, but in some cases, when those planets make the direct aspects with traditional celestial bodies, then they can play major roles in the life of the native.

# Uranus

Everything is sudden and everything is unusual when it comes to this planet. The gift of discoveries, technological breakthroughs, reforms of society and many more traits belong to Uranus. He can be the visionary, although his looks show someone coming from the plain origin. Newness through revolution is his signature. On the negative side, this is a person who is prone to collective trends and thought patterns, a destroyer of an aristocracy, the announcer of catastrophes and triumphs. Prometheus is his real name, for better and for worse. He rules over electricity, x-rays and IT technologies. And regarding traditional astrology, Uranus is seen as the "higher octave" of the planet Mercury. You can say freely – Mercury on steroids. Color is light blue, silver, any metallic shade.

In good planetary aspects with Neptune, this planet shows global trends, gifted mystics, faith, esoteric sciences, ideals of love and humanity, enthusiasm, heavenly music. Negative aspects bring out the fight against the norms and conventions, fall of idols and teachings, political fallacies, sexual disorders and adventurism which can lead to serious danger.

Pluto and Uranus together are never even close to the image of a harmless couple. This is the electricity combined with nuclear power, magicians, yogis, secret medicine, energy healing, scalar waves, tunneling through dimensions, mystical cults, poisoning, occult, psychiatrists, manias in all positive or negative sense of those words, although in those cases there is nothing even close to being considered as pure "positive" or "negative". It's just amazing in its creativity or destruction.

# Neptune

The god of the sea…of illusion. Traditionally seen as the higher octave of the planet Venus and therefore considered as something beyond beautiful, inspirational, delicate beyond perception, magically and sparkling rhythmical, glitter not gold. He also possesses the gift of demonic intuition, the gift of abstract thinking, higher philosophy related to natural sciences, diving into the depths of the sea, of the sky, cosmos, cells, biochemical processes. On the negative side, and yes, Neptune has a negative side as all other planets, this is the generic model of a liar, deceiver, a fraud, fake preacher, fake love, fake faith, fake education. It also had the tendency toward hoaxes, however, it's hard to fight with him. How can you fight fog? When and if got caught, he plays confused. All drugs are here, legal or illegal, all smoking tendencies, bacterial infections, poisoned water, poisoned air.

With any other planet Neptune achieves the miraculous initial success, enchantment and romance follow and then everything ends with disappointment, shame, dishonor, and blasphemy. Together with Pluto, this is poison, extremely high potency poison. Everything is ruined and covered with an indelible layer of pure venom which will last forever, like the consequence of nuclear explosion. In positive aspects, this is the sign of greatest mystic there is, a magician or someone who is dancing on the edge of divine devotion and total craziness.

# PLUTO

The god of the underworld, many call him "fatum". He is the blackest of all black in color, he is the husband of the most beautiful woman and he rules over corpses. Without him, and her, the outer world can't be awakened, can't bloom and reproduce. On our ancestors, we all stand, from the roots we all grow. He is our origin, he is a resurrection, and he will be the end. Small, but dangerous like the energy in the single atom, like a nucleus, like nuclear. Pluto is considered to be the higher octave of the planet Mars and you can come pretty close to the right characteristics of this planet if you imagine it as the Mars with a genius mind and weapons powerful beyond anything else in the Universe...or perhaps Multiverse.

Pluto won't show its powers in any chart. It has to be positioned in angular houses (first, fourth, seventh and tenth) or to make a significant aspect with other planets. In those cases, you can see its powers, but even if you do, you'll wish you didn't.

# NORTH AND SOUTH NODES OF THE MOON

North Node of the Moon is known as the Dragon's head and the South Node of the Moon is known as the Dragon's tail and those are traditional western names for the two calculative points in the sky. In Vedic astrology, those points are known as Rahu and Ketu and further on in this text, they will be addressed by those names, because this is widely spread all over the astrological world.

Rahu, as the North Node, and Ketu, as the South Node, are two opposite points in the chart and these points are the markers where the path of the Moon is crossing the ecliptic belt. These are not celestial bodies and they are always exactly 180 degrees apart from each other.

Myths associate Rahu as the head without the body, while Ketu is the body without the head. Rahu is something we have to process and learn during this current life, while Ketu is something we have already mastered through many of our lives, or in the previous life, which is important for this life in the terms of karma. Of course, if you believe in karma.

Those points tend to become very powerful when they are joined with planets in natal charts and they are capable of creating real havoc or powerful blessing, depending on other planetary aspects, and coming solar and lunar eclipses regarding transits.

Eclipses happen due to the fact that Sun and Moon are together on one of those two points or they are in opposition on the Rahu-Ketu axis. They bring changes; they take some things, issues, ideas or people we no longer need from us and present us with new events, people, issues, and ideas, whether we want this to happen or not. This is the nature of life, constant changes and growth through those changes.

Eclipses happening on the natal Sun can indicate a new direction in life, the danger for the father, while the eclipsed Moon can represent the danger for the mother or the soul of the native. Venus associated with Nodes will always bring unresolved issues into your love life and great instability with women, while similar can be applied for Mars, but in the terms of activity, men, enthusiasm. When the Nodes are placed together with Jupiter, a person will always seek higher knowledge, transform and adopt new teachings. With Saturn and Nodes joined in the natal chart, a person will feel cursed until the hard lessons about life, health, career, and discipline are mastered completely.

Association between Uranus, Neptune, and Pluto with Rahu or Ketu will always point in the direction of scientific, artistic or technological breakthroughs and those people will certainly have to go through many challenges, but at the same time, they will feel the strong, driving force to carry on and they don't give up on their dreams.

# HOW TO READ THE ASTROLOGICAL

# CHART

Simply put, an astrological chart is the projection of the sky on the Earth's plane. Of course, that the Earth is not a plane, but this is not the question here because we approximate the image of the sky onto ourselves as if we were the center of the world. And if we "catch" the image of the sky at the same moment we were born, then we have the "natal chart". The same is applicable for the charts of the animals, buildings, companies, business deals, events like weddings, receptions and anything you can think of. These are all natal charts and they all describe the potential for good and bad events, which can happen further on, depending on some other factors.

The main one of those "other factors" are planetary transits. They are the most important fact in western astrology; while the Vedic school favors divisional charts, which is an arrangement of the planets and sensitive points in the chart calculated through some geometrical and mathematical rules. However, we will discuss the western or tropical school of astrology here. To avoid confusion, you should know that Vedic or sidereal astrology deals with sidereal positions of the planets in the sky, while western astrology deals with tropical positions or the projection of planets on the Earth's plane. In simple words, for example, the first day of spring is March 21st. We know this because day and night are equal and this is called the spring equinox. The Sun enters into the sign of Aries and the new cycle begins. You know that this is the equinox; you know that spring is here, but if you go to the observatory and look at the Sun through a telescope, you will see that Sun is still in the constellation of Pisces. This "effect" is happening due to the precession of the equinoxes; however, for now this concept is beyond the basics of astrology.

The most important thing you have to know is that both astrological schools are right, they have their precise prediction systems, which differ, but they both work. The quality of the prediction depends on the quality of chosen astrologer, not the school which is selected for the reading.

Let's get back to planetary transits. This is the term which describes the image of the current or upcoming planetary arrangement in the sky. If you, for instance, overlap the transit chart over your natal chart, you will be able to see the areas where you are challenged, blessed, where can you grow, in what to invest, from what or who to beware and so on. Sometimes the warning signs are extremely obvious if you know how to read those two sets of planetary arrangements together.

The same applies to your partner's charts, whether they can show the development and the outcome of love, business or any other relationship. All you need to do is to overlap those two charts and to read mutual aspects that the planets make.

# GENERAL ASTROLOGY RULES

First, you have to know the meaning of each planet and the meaning of each astrological sign. Then you have to know the basic aspects planets make together.

The chart in the western astrology style is presented as a circle divided into 12 parts, each one representing astrological houses. The most important points are the Ascendant – Descendant (Asc-Dsc) line, which is a horizontal line in the chart and the Medium Coeli – Imum Coeli (MC-IC) line, which is showing the highest and the lowest points of your chart. Those are four of the most important points you have to pay attention to. Asc is your rising sign, describing just you. Dsc is how you deal with your love, business or any other partner and how you project yourself into the world. IC is your origin, while MC is your highest accomplishment.

A circle with the cross in it, it is so simple, and the whole life in it.

The image of your natal chart will look like this circle, but with the snapshot of the planetary arrangements at the moment you were born. This snapshot holds the potentials which will develop to a greater or a lesser degree, depending on upcoming planetary transits during your life. Whether those potentials and life's events are good or bad, you will know by reading the aspects the planets make.

# PLANETARY ASPECTS

Whenever celestial body moves through the heavens, it creates a motion, therefore frequency, and therefore sound. Any relation between celestial bodies creates a mutual aspect and all together they make the music of the spheres. However, the aspects considered as the most important in astrology are conjunction, sextile, square, trine and opposition.

Conjunction happens when the two planets are placed close to each other so their influences are mixed. If there are three or more planets involved, then this is called stellium. Are the planets forming conjunction or stellium? This depends on their orbs of influences. Bigger bodies have greater orbs and for the Sun, Moon, Jupiter, and Saturn, this can extend to 15 degrees because they are big planets with great strength. Also, depending on the planets involved, conjunction can be considered as good or bad.

Sextile is formed between planets when they form the 60-degree angle between them looking from the center point of an astrological circle or a chart. Generally speaking, this is a good aspect and suggests that planets are active and can result in a positive outcome.

Square happens when two planets form a 90-degree angle in the chart and squares are often perceived as bad aspects because they can bring very challenging situations in our lives. But, at the same time, they force us to change and to grow in attempts to overcome or resolve our problems.

Trine is seen as the exceptionally auspicious aspect and it happens when two planets form a 120-degree angle between them. Although beneficial, trines can sometimes produce a lazy attitude, so there is really nothing just black and white going on in the sky.

An opposition is another "bad" aspect because two celestial bodies are forming 180-degrees angle and they are directly opposing each other. This is challenging too, causing open war between opposite sides, frictional, but at the same time, it provokes the search for a better option or solution.

# ZODIAC SIGNS AND HOUSES

Now that we have learned the general meaning of planets and aspects in the chart, we should take the closer look at the astrological signs and houses. As you already know, the horoscope is divided into four sectors (remember the cross in the circle?) and twelve "houses" or main areas of life. In Vedic astrology, those houses are equal. Each one extends to 30 degrees. However, in the western school, this is not the case, because the geometry of the point on Earth where you were born, for instance, is calculated through various systems. This is something which is beyond the basics, but you should know that today, Placidus house system is mostly used and it shows the best results, except in the case that person was born in the areas of polar circles.

The main rule of astrology is that each Zodiac sign has the meaning of the same house. Translated, this rule can be easily explained looking at the signs. Aries is the first sign in the Zodiac belt, so the first house of any horoscope has the general meaning of the sign of Aries; the second house has the meaning of Taurus and so on until we reach to the Pisces or twelfth house.

For instance, you can be born in the sign of Gemini and this means that you were born between the 21st of May until 20th of June. However, if you were born, let's say, during the afternoon hours, your rising sign or your Ascendant could be placed in the sign of Scorpio. This is just an example; we will have to know the exact time to see where the Ascendant is placed.

Now, you have your natal Sun in Gemini, but your rising sign is Scorpio. This means that your first house is placed in the sign of Scorpio, but at the same time, this means that you will have all the traits of Aries (first house) through the characteristics of Scorpio. In this case, also, the Sun is placed in Gemini, but in the eighth house of the horoscope, which again carries the symbolism of the sign of Scorpio. Add to this mix the position of your natal Moon and you will have the basic understanding of your character and appearance.

It can sound a bit complicated for an absolute beginner, but in time and with the little practice, you will start using those "double" systems, not even thinking about them while applying the rules.

Right now, have in mind that Hor, Horus or Hrs is the son of the god of time and this word can be found in many Indo-European languages and also in Egypt. Horoscope was the name for the priest who controls the measuring of the time. "Horos-scopein" means literally the clock watcher. Horoscope is all about the flow of time through the certain place, but is this the driving force through entire Universe?

Let's find out.

# ARIES

Sun transits through Aries from the 21st of March until the 21st of April and during this period of time, the Sun increases its power rapidly, nature is awakening and suddenly we feel the urge to take action.

The sign of Aries or the first house in the chart is all about me, ego, will. The ruler of this sign is the planet Mars, which is diurnal (through daytime), this is also the male sign, the element is fire and the color is red. Aries is the cardinal sign and planet Mars rules Tuesday. Countries under this sign are Germany, Japan, Israel, Syria, Poland.

Aries is the image of the perfect soldier. He is strong, determined, a patriot, skilled in the art of war. He is also fast, with a rudimentary type of will, one-sided in his thinking, but honest and often naïve. With the strong constitution and proper training – he is extremely dangerous. His favorite places are open spaces for sporting or martial arts activities, stadiums, city centers, all tall and new buildings made of steel and glass.

His feelings are fiery, passionate, easily affected, always above reasoning. His commitment to love can last for a very short or very long time, depending on the levels of passion he receives from his partner. In business, he needs some time to get the "rules of the game", but when he incorporates them then the breakthroughs are made. As a worker, he is very loyal, but tends to create tremendous stress and needs the time for relaxing after.

His best professions are related to sports, military, engineering, metallurgy, surgeries and any other type of duty where responsibility, clear line of command, order, and activity are necessary. He loves uniforms of any sort, no matter whether those uniforms are of the military and medical nature. He will equally enjoy the "uniform" of his favorite sports club, or him being dressed as a butcher, electrician, plumber or any other profession he is in.

There is no need to suppress this grandiose energy or Martian rage, especially when it comes to children born in the sing of the Ram. It's better to channel it through sports and activities in nature. Aries natives need to eat healthily, drink a lot of pure water and to spend their time in open spaces under the Sun. They should keep out of the stale atmosphere, small spaces, and boring environments.

Young women tend to be insecure because they are uncertain about the levels of their energy. They can be perceived as too strong and this ruins their chances for romance. And romance they want, indeed, like we all do. In this case, they feel better in groups and for them, and all other younger Aries natives, it's imperative to use the powerful inner drive creatively, because if they don't - they will tend to become members or even the leaders of delinquency groups.

Marriage for Aries people happens early and if their partner is calm in nature or prone to more feminine energies, this union will last for a lifetime because they need someone to be their safe fortress when they come back home. They are faithful because they are unable to lie and even if they fall in love beside their official partner, they will break this affair pretty quickly or they will divorce fast and remarry even faster. The sign of Ram is about honesty, even when it's based on naivety; about newness and rebirth. Strong outside, but very soft inside, the Ram is brave, interested in everything around him and careless like a baby.

The natives are not insensitive, as others could start to think; they are just bursting with energy and usually joy and precisely because they are so sensitive deep down inside, they cover their softness with the shield of sports, martial arts or membership of any organized group.

Sun exalts here in the sign of the Ram or in the first house of the horoscope because the Sun is the king and king just loves to show off leading his armies to war. This is the clear sign of very strong ego, self-sustaining type of thinking and living habits. In positive aspects with other planets, this is the characteristic of a psychologically strong native with a heightened sense of justice. However, when afflicted this Sun can show a tendency to become the dictator, he will certainly be inadequate when it comes to compromising and prone to quarreling, jealousy and simply unbearable. It can also indicate injuries of the eyes.

The Moon is seen as "too dried out" in this sign because the nature of the Moon is to be cold and moist and in those circumstances, the Moon is left on the hot and dry surface. A person with the Moon in the first house or placed in Aries will tend to have a short temper, sometimes brisk attitude and often be insensitive toward other's emotions. Injuries of the eyes (dry eyes) show in this case too, but together with the hurt feelings.


Mercury feels good wherever he resides, or at least he thinks so. This small planet of communication here doesn't know when to stop and words, words, words are spilled all around, often said in a rude manner or through an irritated tone. Agitator, a messenger in war, but good for sports, especially group sports like basketball, volleyball and similar activities.

Planet Venus is in detriment in the sign of Aries. This doesn't mean that she is losing her powers; it's simply the sign that she doesn't feel good here. Short hair, red hair, red lipstick, red clothes, sometimes sloppy and not so finely paired, sports shoes with the dress, elegant handbag with yoga pants, she can make great fashion designers cry out of sadness or a joy, depending on the positions of other planets. This is also the only position of Venus which indicates a turnaround in the game of love. Woman pursues a man, or in the case of male's horoscope, he waits to be pursued by a woman. For gay couples, this means that the one with dominant female's energy pursues the one with the dominant male's energy.

Mars is in his home here. Strong and powerful, but hard to handle. It also points into the direction of constant stress, even strokes, injuries of the head, especially the nose, redness in the face and body and often, scars. Blond and reddish blond, curly hair. Mars in Aries or in the first house rules the head - the skull (but without the lower jaw) and the hair.

Jupiter placed in the first house or in the sign of Aries shows joyous temperament, prone to weight gains, fatty cheeks and round eyes. An enthusiastic person, highly educated if other planetary positions are supportive and this is the image of the military priest or military doctor.

Saturn is in fall in Aries or in the first house. This indicates a very stubborn person, overwhelmed with life's changes. The danger of loss of hearing, injury to ears, problems with the upper teeth and even brain tumors. Stressful search for justice, for peace, for rest.

Uranus in Aries and also in the first house is the sudden explosion with long-lasting consequences. Unusual mind or methodology of thinking, "out of the box" solutions when Uranus is positively supported by the other planets, and a harsh and even crazy character in challenging positions. Use of the newest frequency types of technologies in engineering or as a weapon. Bipolar disorders, a pressure in the eyes, nervous breakdowns.

Neptune in Aries can be the true disaster. This is the planet of illusions, so in such dry theater of war operations, this planet is lost in alcohol and drugs. This can also point toward secret and popular "sports" among soldiers which include some sort of religious devotion mixed with drugs, most likely illegal ones. Generally, it can show problems with eyes, like cataracts, dementia, but also the talents for acting. In good aspects, this points toward hydraulics and pneumatics, new engineering technologies when it comes to water, oil or gases.

Pluto in Aries or in the first house is all about resurrection. Independent fanatic spirit, strong will and volcanic types of instincts. Demonic attraction and mad courage, black magic, fall, unique history.

# TAURUS

The Sun transits through the sign of Taurus from the 21st of April until the 21st of May and during this time frame the Sun is stabilizing, everything in nature is ready for propagation. This is the time of quiet excitement, love, pleasure.

The sign of Taurus or the second house in the chart is all about mine, properties, belongings. The ruler of this sign is the planet Venus, which is here nocturnal (through nighttime) according to Ptolemy's Table of Essential Dignities; this is also the female sign, the element is the earth and the colors are brown and green. Taurus is the fixed sign and the planet Venus rules Friday. Countries under this sign are Ireland, Switzerland, Cuba, Tanzania, Cyprus.

Taurus is a female sign and that is why is easier to think of her as one very healthy and strong woman coming from the natural environment. She is slow and meticulous, but steady and she gets her work done. Someone might think that she is not so bright, but her slowness is far from being dumb. She knows the value of everything in every moment and this is why the sign of Bull is so important for monetary transactions.

She holds the keys to all rooms on her property and in every second she knows how much money her family possesses and where will expenses appear and how will the profits be made.

She is traditional and yes, she is the essence of value.

In medical terms, Taurus rules over the neck, thyroid gland, many hormones and lower jaw. Natives born in this sign tends to accumulate weight through life and if this is the case with women, many of them will have to starve their bodies to remain near the looks of a modern ideal of beauty. However, many of those women just give up and they enjoy this accumulation of everything, including fat.

Marriages last for a lifetime and many times love is being born out of the pure calculation, which is absolutely nothing bad in the eyes of one Taurus because substantial resources are the only guarantee for the happy ever after. How can we talk about love when I haven't seen your properties? How will I ever think of starting a family with you if you don't have enough money? What do you expect – to keep my future children hungry? These are all very realistic question one Taurus will think about even on the first date.

Children of this sign are peaceful and they desperately need the time spent outside in nature. You will raise them the best if you keep them playing on the meadow, in the woods, near the animals. And let them work all farmers' types of jobs or let them experiment in the kitchen. They won't all be involved in agriculture, but many of them will become the great biologists, especially botanists, builders, architects, exclusive cooks, animal trainers, veterinarians. But on the other side, this world of matter will make out of many of them respected bankers, investors, industrialists, high profile managers. Don't worry about their future, because they will be capable to raise their kingdom even if they don't possess a thing in the beginning.

The Sun generally feels good in the sign of Taurus or placed in the second house of the horoscope. This is all about incomes and all about earning money in style. However, profits are in most cases made through the land, farming, especially fruits and vegetables, although raising stock is also popular among these natives. Every business deal is checked first with parents, parental figures or a spouse. Tradition is important and respected through generations. Strong neck, strong voice.

The Moon just loves to be in Taurus. This is the place where the Moon exalts because it deals with security and family fortune. It's so easy to feel good when food is plenty, the land is fertile, stables are full of animals and rooms are full of children. Harmony and love. Big sensitive eyes, women tend to gain weight easily, especially in the second part of life, and there could be some problems with the thyroid gland. It's necessary for the person with any planet in this sign, especially the Moon, to walk bare feet on the ground.

Mercury is a bit slow here. It takes time to form the sentence, to think, to read. He doesn't even want to bother with those things when calculating profits and expenses are his favorite activities. Geometry is perhaps something too complicated to deal with, but when it comes to other mathematical areas like the stock market, Taurus Mercury can be invincible. When placed well, this indicates that the person loves to sing those old witty folk songs or the native has a natural gift for hip-hop reciting. Nice incomes from several small sources.

Venus is the fairy queen here. She is the best looking girl in the whole county and perhaps even further. This is her kingdom and she feels good in her body, in her home, in her properties, and with her own money. In many cases, she has a magical voice and singing is her natural talent. When receiving some negative aspects, this Venus can behave a bit like a sugar baby. Over the course of years, as her fortune increases, her weight will increase too. There are so many cases when a woman with this position is famous in the world of entertainment, has everything, but starves deliberately because her body accumulates everything. She adores designer's pieces in fashion, elegant clothes and extremely expensive handbags, shoes, and jewelry.

Mars is in his sign of detriment in Taurus. He doesn't lose his power, but he feels lazy and defeated by the fullness of life. There are no wars to fight in the rich land of eternal spring. He is like the soldier on his days off, so he just lies on the ground, looking at the sky or checking if any of the village girls walk nearby. He is also the great chef here and he is known for his meals made out of meat. Royal nutrition, yes, he also gains weight easily, but his body is big and covered in muscles. He loves woods and he finds his talents through working as a carpenter or peasant here. In the second house of horoscope, Mars creates expenses, usually for the home and personal items, but still expenses.

Jupiter in Taurus or placed in the second house can bring fortune, but this will happen only if the native is honest, educated and well prepared. This planet behaves like the omen from heavens here, but only if the ground is prepared in advance. Methodical techniques in agriculture bring success and methodical thinking goes the long way with Jupiter in the house of incomes.

Saturn in Taurus can indicate poverty in a very shallow sense of understanding astrology. This is happening because the influences of Jupiter and Saturn are misunderstood. Jupiter is the fortune, but the fortune in a spiritual or educational sense, while Saturn is the one to symbolize wealth in the terms of real, material properties. In this particular case the native can start poor and end rich, or the native can possess the ability to find cheap or to inherit something insignificant and turn it into a fortune. Great position for surface mining, archeology, sculpting, turning old peasant houses and farms into exclusive retreats. Good for banking also.

Uranus in Taurus is all about stock market changes, new agricultural technologies, disrupted currencies and economic crises. When Uranus is placed in the second house triggered by the other planetary transits it can create sudden gains or sudden losses of wealth.

Neptune in Taurus is all about trying to put down the heavens on the earth. In the positive context, this relates to art. A person is capable of making or singing heavenly music; this is innovation regarding sculpting and also amazing architecture. Someone might discover a geyser on the property, but on the negative side, this is extreme sensitivity toward chemicals and the danger of choking. Monetary gains through cheating.

Pluto in Taurus is great for forensics. This is all about digging bodies, digging knowledge, digging precious artifacts. It's also the demonic power of the Earth itself and some very weird ways of earning money while dancing on the edge of the law.

# GEMINI

The Sun transits through the sign of Gemini from the 21st of May until the 20th of June and during this time frame, the Sun is playful and communicative. This is the time of information exchange, sharing, exploring.

The sign of Gemini or the third house in the chart is all about the joy of belonging to a group, sharing, showing, marketing. The ruler of this sign is the planet Mercury, which is here diurnal (through daytime) according to Ptolemy's Table of Essential Dignities. This is also the male sign, the element is the air and the colors are yellow, orange and all pastel shades. Gemini is the mutable sign and planet Mercury rules Wednesday. Countries under this sign are Belgium, Iceland, Kuwait, Tunisia.

Organs under Mercury's or Gemini's government are hands, lungs, and brain (together with Jupiter). He is all about neurology, transport of information through the body, its logistics. These are the processes where the sign of Gemini is beyond being just shallow because it shows our capacity to breathe and to distribute the nutritious matter through the whole body.

Natives born under the sign of Twins in most cases have a sibling and very close relationship with them. Besides this fact, they are always surrounded by numerous friends and although those friendships are very changeable in nature, natives continue to grow the enormous circle of acquaintances. It's very important to know the proper person for a proper issue; this is the leading motive for any Gemini.

Their marriages or relationships are mostly far from being committed at least in their younger years. Later on, when other planets become dominant factors in their chart they can become faithful, but before this happens they have to live and relive the experiences of feeling joyous with multiple people. The usual case is two marriages, one which happened too early and was driven by passion and ruined by impatience, and the second one which happened when native started to feel old and realized that everyone around is in a committed relationship.

One unusual, but very common thing going on for young Twins is the fact that most of them have to go through very serious illnesses as babies and those health problems are frequently related to lungs or breathing in general. There is always some sort of drama going on in children's hospitals and after the hardest first year of life, everything that follows looks much better. Young Twins are very cheerful children, so joyous that you'll get often headaches just looking at them. They enjoy elementary school and all childish games and they want to stay in this protected land of childhood forever.

Just don't force them to learn about complicated sciences and thing of the past, because it will be extremely difficult for them to understand and totally useless for their careers. Good profession for Gemini natives is a journalist, marketer, teacher, instructor, reporter, editor, writer, seller, trader, lawyer. Others might complain that these are not so grandiose professions like being an architect or chemist, but without these professions, our world would stop. Someone needs to be the messenger between people and gods after all.

The Sun in Gemini or in the third house of the horoscope is all about the speech, imagination, skills, expertize, but regarding down to earth knowledge which is applicable in every day's life. This is also the game, the art of trading, exchanging any sort of information or assets, practicality, and intellectualism. Established in the sign of Aries and secured by Taurus, the Sun is now like a little child ready to explore the neighborhood. Everything is new and exciting and worth researching.

The Moon in Gemini or placed in the third house describes the restless soul and spirit. I want to be here and there, in the best case scenario, at the same time and I love to hear about this and that, mostly nothing important, but it doesn't matter. People with the Moon positioned like this love to drive around the city, frequent short travels and fast food places, especially the street sold foods. Their relationship with their mother looks like a teenager friendship and communication is flowing free, but mostly about non-essential issues.

Mercury in Gemini or in the third area of the chart is in his own place. This is the image of an investigative journalist, speculative trader, entrepreneur, marketer, someone who works with children, like teachers in elementary schools and kindergartens. It's all about the play of life, all about bubbling and chatting and building something new seamlessly out of nothing, i.e., magazines, newspapers, websites, nothing too deep. When positioned negatively, this Mercury indicates mental problems, Autism Spectrum Disorder or ASD, even bipolar behavior.

Venus in Gemini is the image of a girl or a boy, or whatever you like her or him to be. Also Venus and Mercury in close or tense aspects with Uranus can indicate a homosexual or bisexual person too. But more important for this Venus is her girly or boyish appearance. Her body is not developed fully like in a grown woman, her legs are long and thin and she is the moment of glory for the fashion industry because every piece of clothing on her looks exactly like when it's on the hanger. She is about parties and gossiping, about shopping and spending her time in cafes and in the city.

Mars in Gemini or placed in the third house is the evident sign for the entrepreneurial spirit. From every penny, he will make two, from any garbage information he will make pure gold. He will raise his empire on marketing, selling fog, selling some shallow educational stuff applicable in business. He will use his power in the world of communication and when involved in construction building he will focus on the downtowns of big cities – small and practical apartments, but in the heart of the world.

This Mars is also exceptionally good when it comes to martial arts instructors, someone who has to teach, explain and fight at the same time. These are strong fists too. And if positioned negatively, this is the small street criminal, punches or slaps.

Jupiter placed in the sign of Gemini is in his sign of detriment; the same applies for the third house in personal horoscopes. This planet doesn't feel good here, because the deep and broad knowledge it carries can't be expressed completely through the certain shallowness of celestial Twins. In good aspects, this indicates someone who is very talented in sports, especially group sports like basketball and some natives seems to grow very tall with this position. Negatively speaking this can lead to some cognitive problems, ASD again, because fats and neurology are not composed properly in the brain tissue.

Saturn in Gemini points to some verbal problems; the person seems too slow, not capable of verbalizing or expressing thoughts fast enough. This also indicates some misunderstandings with siblings, especially younger ones, troubles with lungs and neurology. This is good for building business in the later part of life, though.

Uranus in Gemini or placed in the third area of the chart is about disruptions of the speech or the ideas. Often bipolar, ASD which can be used in the world of new communication technologies, odd ideas, new solutions, out of the box type of thinking if other aspects are confirming the strength of Uranus. This is good for electricians, online speakers, TV reporters. It also indicates some sudden events in the life of native which will take place in the neighborhood or nearby, when other transits trigger this planetary placement.

Neptune in Gemini is the symbol for a great writer or a liar depending on other aspects, but it's usually both. Something odd can happen in the neighborhood, a person gets inspired while walking or talking with neighbors. Strange events inspire this person, they are mindful of mythical inspiration,

117

this is great for poets and science fiction novelists. At the same time, a person with Neptune in the third house will always find a church or any religious temple near his/her home and he/she will go there frequently no matter what is his/her religious background may be.

Pluto in Gemini is cunning, sly, witty, and tricky above everything else. This is the omen for the magnificent manipulator, someone who does horrible things in a childish manner. They have unusual intelligence, but it is always accompanied with sarcasm.

# CANCER

The Sun transits through the sign of Cancer from the 21st of June until the 22nd of July and during this period of time, the Sun is about nurturing, home and motherly figures. This is the symbol for taking care, being intuitive and sensitive.

The sign of Cancer or the fourth house has the main theme of inner protection, safety provided by family and ancestral origin. The ruler of this sign is the Moon, which is here both diurnal and nocturnal according to Ptolemy's Table of Essential Dignities. This is also the female sign, the element is the water and the colors are blue, silver and all pearly shades. Cancer is the cardinal sign and the Moon rules during Monday. Countries under this sign are USA, Holland, Madagascar, and Bahamas.

Organs under the Moon's or Cancer's rulership are stomach, breasts, and womb, but in the case when the baby is inside the mother. This is also the symbol for the egg in a woman or any animal. This is the flow of water inside of us and therefore, it's imperative for females. Any organ filled with water becomes the Moon's belonging in those moments of fullness.

This is the symbol for big, watery eyes, commonly blue, babies and nutrition. Any pregnant woman is under the rulership of the Moon. Moodiness is a frequent flow of emotions, extreme sensitivity, night time, lakes, greater water surface with the full Moon mirroring in it, mirrors, tears, pearls. Constant changes in incomes, schedules, feelings. Good for dairy production, taking care of children, babies, nursing, taking care of elderly people, running restaurants, hotels, hostels.

The Sun in Cancer or placed in the fourth house of the chart describes sensitive person attached to mother, family or ancestors in general. Patriotism is strong here, although the Sun doesn't show his powers openly. This represents the nation, national pride, and heritage. Everything which deals with ideas of helping others through genuine care will be shown through this Sun. Perhaps it's too soft, but this Sun is not weak in the sign of Crab, it just doesn't want to show off and parade as it does in other signs. Their place of residence looks humble from the outside, but marvelous inside.

This Moon in Cancer is in its own house. This Moon feels protected and there is a clear lineage of women ancestors from whom the native learns about life, care, and support. This is the symbol of fertility, but at the same time, it indicates the frequent moves of the entire family. The kitchen is the prominent place for family gathering and many meals are based on milk, cheese and especially butter. The native with this placement knows how to heal members of the family, specifically children, with warm milk with spices and honey, soups, and teas. Although attached to the home, this native will often move to new locations and he will tend to settle down beside a lake or a larger pond.

Mercury placed in this sign of the fourth house indicates that person is very attached to the home, gains "down to earth" every day's knowledge usually from the mother, many people are transiting through the home, neighbors, friends, house full of siblings. There is a lot of information exchanged through mother or home environment, good for people who are working remotely online. They want small apartments, but close to the center of cities, small kitchens, small chairs or rooms, small items.

Venus in Cancer or placed in the fourth house of horoscope usually portraits the woman with big eyes, round face, bigger breasts, prone to weight gains due to excess water in her body. She is sensitive, focused on family, nurturing, somewhat conservative. Loves romance, nice items, nice manners. This is the symbol for the hidden mother in any woman, a lot of female friends, love can be found in the home through a visitor. She values security above all and she will be faithful in any sense of the word, to any man who is protecting her. Her complete soul will belong to her family.

Mars in Cancer or specially placed in the fourth house is in its fall here. Generally speaking, this is the worst position for the warrior. Just imagine the situation of letting the soldier take care of a baby, or letting a heavily armed warrior in the kitchen. His nature is fiery and he will cause all sorts of disputes in the home. In personal relationships, this is the image of a couple in a constant fight, verbal or physical. The man can abuse his wife, but at the same time, his whole family. The same goes for an aggressive woman. Fiery weapons held in the home, the danger of shooting, the danger of something burning in the kitchen, constant danger of fires. In the best case scenario, this is the person who constantly does some repairs or improvements in the home, so the drilling and breaking of the walls are a never-ending annoying sound for the entire family. And because Mars is so weak here, the native can become the bravest one, because he/she had to learn how to fight with everyone from the earliest age. Hot foods, stomachache, and a metabolism so fast that it tends to burn out the body earlier in life.

Jupiter in Cancer and divinely placed in the fourth house is in the sign of its exaltation. It's the common belief that this Jupiter can bring the expansion of the family's properties and wealth in general, but the truth is somewhat different than just this one aspect. This is the sign of exaltation for the big celestial guru, because higher knowledge should be inherited from the mother and female lineage in the family. From an early age, the mother should be the one to teach her children about fine manners, ability to listen and to feel, to absorb positive information, good foods, and stable emotions. This is the excellent position to feel protected from the inside, because Mars and the Sun are in charge of the outer protection, fighting and winning in the male style. Jupiter placed here is all about refined education and the healthy educational and intellectual abilities derived from healthy food and having a healthy mother. This is also the sign that properties are huge, food is plentiful and the surrounding area of the home is reflecting nature, meaning that there are lots of parks there, areas for sporting activities and even a temple related to the religion of origin.

Saturn in Cancer is in the sign of his detriment, unfortunately. This indicates obstacles in relation to the mother, chronic diseases, usually derived from sensitive stomach, problems with digestion, allergies to dairy, allergies to everything which came from the female lineage. Problems with heating, a person is often cold and catches colds in the house, the cold and dry atmosphere among the members of the family, growing up with grandparents and in many cases, the grandmother takes the role of the mother. This is a good position for producing ice-creams, distilled drinks, creating an exclusive retreat out of the old property, vineries, houses made of stones.

Uranus in Cancer announces frequent changes regarding home, moving in a sudden manner, a lot of uncertainty, neurotic mother, problems with electricity, irregular digestion, irregular childhood, growing amongst "crazy" or at least unusual people, growing beside electricity plant, problems with electricity, electrical devices behave out of control, especially in the kitchen, someone experiments with all sorts of technical items in the home, inventors, disruptors.

Neptune in the sign of Crab or placed in the fourth house of the chart indicates very foggy problems at home. The mother could have some eyesight issues; there could be an alcoholic always present, if not at home, then one of the close neighbors is prone to addiction of some sort, words and emotions are not clear, floods coming from the bathroom, spilled milk, always something boiling with the danger of exploding. Someone practicing homeopathy or creating pharmaceutical drugs from home. Home factory of illegal drugs, tarot card readers, something chemical or alchemical always going on. Frequent problems with bacterial infection and food poisoning. Some good advice is to avoid mushrooms.

Pluto in Cancer or placed in the fourth house indicates that some sort of the criminal act was done regarding ancestors. There could be a body buried underneath the home or around the property. A sudden explosion, crime, murder. On the positive side of this aspect, the native can discover a hidden treasure or any sort hiding in his home or origin.

# LEO

The Sun transits through the sign of Leo from the 22nd of July until the 23rd of August and during this period of time the Sun is about dignity, pride, and domination. This is the symbol for royalty, entertainment, and children.

The sign of Leo or the fifth house is all about ruling over others, being just and doing well. The ruler of this sign is the Sun, which is here both diurnal and nocturnal according to Ptolemy's Table of Essential Dignities. This is the male sign, the element is the fire and the colors are yellow, gold and all glittery shades. Leo is the fixed sign and the Sun rules during Sunday. Countries under this sign are France, Italy, Mongolia, Bolivia.

Organs under the Sun's or Leo's rulership are the heart, spine and bone marrow. This is also the symbol of the life itself because the Sun is the light or the fire within. Natives born in this sign almost never get cancer of any kind and they manage to eliminate diseases very fast. However, they are in the greater danger of having a heart attack.

Odd but true, Leo has two sides of his character. He is like a child, enthusiastic about everything, open-minded and always in a good mood – he shines like the Sun. On the other side, he is the great organizer, structured and orderly leader with the clear set of intentions and instructions. He loves tradition and national history, he exalts in luxury, but only when he is the one, the alpha. He is the big hearted and large-minded individual with the established sense of hierarchy.

This native resolves all disputes in gentleman's manner, there is no point for jealousy because he/she is the best one and if the love partner is not clear or doesn't understand this, native will just leave with pride to find someone else who will respect him/her more. Marriage usually happens in the middle age when he had already accomplished something grand in his own life and this marriage is usually with the "trophy partner".

Children of the Lion are courageous and they should spend their times together with others learning to treat everyone equally. With afflicted planets, these children tend to gain weight very early in life.

The Sun in Leo or placed in the fifth house of horoscope is the basic image of the king (or queen), good heritage, dignity, and honesty. This is the person with strong principles and ordered mind, someone who loves formalism, good manners and open and honest conversation. In the negative context, this can also point toward snobbism, vanity or arrogance. This person has bright, often light eyes, greyish, wide forehead, curly hair, and strong stature. Later in life, the native is prone to become stubby. She has a talent for acting, drama, entertainment, and humor in general. Childish, but with the pure heart and this is the image of a child wanting to rule the whole world. Coat of arms, lions, flags, parades, bees, baroque – they all belong to Leo and the mighty Sun.

The Moon in Leo or placed in the fifth house can be a bit dried out when it comes to emotions. Feelings are present, but they are covered with a sense of duty and common sense. The native feels great love toward children and enjoys the idea to have many of them, but this is also the sign of having just one child in most cases. However, this is the wonderful placement for entertainment industry or working as the teacher in elementary school. There is increased flow through the heart, but a mobile spine at the same time.

Mercury in the sign of Leo or placed in the fifth area of the chart is the gift of a great speaker, especially when it comes to motivation. This Mercury is capable to mobilize masses from their depressive state of mind into any adventures, to make them go to war, build the fortress or calm down. These are also all expensive vehicles and the children of the rich people, who are capable of expanding the industries of their parents or just to enjoy their fortune and without fail to record experiences of a luxury life through social media.

Venus in the sign of Leo is always dressed to impress. She is branded from head to toe, and even if she doesn't possess means to wear expensive items yet, she will find some appropriate clothes which will resemble her dream to be dominant. This is the symbol for gold, exquisite jewelry, high heeled shoes with red soles, and small handbags with golden or platinum credit cards inside. Usually, her hair is long and blond, and she tries to keep her body in the best shape as long as she can. A native with this position of Venus finds love in the places of celebration, theaters or receptions. This is someone who will appear just in quality or luxury places and search for the adequate partner. Reason is leading the feelings and even when the third party gets involved, the native resolves the unpleasant situation without jealousy by just leaving in dignity.

Mars in Leo or in the fifth house indicates the soldier who wants to show off. This is the leader on the military parade. The pompous king who lives for adoration coming from his people. This is the portrait of a person who needs to be on the top and who will do anything to get there. At the same time, this indicates troubles with heart, easy exhaustion, passion and rage for life which can easily turn into weakness or illness. Good for practicing sports though.

Jupiter in Leo or placed in the fifth house is a person with a big heart in the positive and negative sense of the word. This could be the marvelous teacher, magnificent actor, someone who loves children and is blessed with very educated and successful progeny. At the same time, in the case that Jupiter receives negative aspects coming from other planets, this can be the person who wants to act like he/she is rich, educated and successful, but in reality, all those attempts fail with public humiliation. This can also be the lottery winners in some cases and problems with fat deposits in the arteries too.

Saturn in Leo is all about longing for progeny because this is the sign of his detriment. Usually, people with this position of Saturn want very passionately to become parents, but their wish comes true later in life and they always tend to have fewer children than they wished for. In bad aspects, this signifies afflictions with children, problematic romances, and a sad love life. Saturn here is also the sign of the great leader or politician, but someone who will have to rise through oppression or he will fall in shame. Changes in politics, turnarounds, turmoil, fall of the royal house.

Uranus in Leo creates special situations. This is someone who comes from the lower social rank and through the ideas of anarchy, communism or social politics tends to ruin the established system only to position him/herself as the next ruler. This is the image for crimes in high society, for exclusive frauds and disruptors of tradition. Placed in the fifth house, Uranus indicates highly unstable love life, frequent relationships with psychologically immature partners and electrically disrupted heart.

Neptune in Leo is the clear sign of an unclear love life. Children might not belong to the native, they could be spurious, or the native could create children and then just disappear from their lives. This is the sign of love affairs; disrupted love life followed with all sorts of sexual disorders, love for illegal substances, especially in the liquid or gas states. This is also an indication of bacterial or viral infection of the heart or something unclear when it comes to heart or spinal function. On the positive side, these are talented musicians or poets.

Pluto placed in the fifth house or in the sign of Leo, if in the significant aspects with other celestial bodies, will create a sudden and great emperor in politics, in business, in entertainment. Everything around this person will be grandiose, destined and doomed. Also, this is the symbol for powerful children, exceptional life force coming straight from the heart, raw behavior, for avatars and gurus with supernatural powers, sudden death, unexplained murder.

# VIRGO

The Sun transits through the sign of Virgo from the 23rd of August until the 23rd of September and during this period of time, the Sun is about collecting the fruits, healing, and serving. This is the symbol for the fullness of the autumn, hard workers, and natural healers.

The sign of Virgo or the sixth house is all about fixing, ordering or editing, being in service and doing the best for others. The ruler of this sign is the planet Mercury, which is here both nocturnal (during the night) according to a Ptolemy's Table of Essential Dignities. This is the female sign, the element is the earth and the colors are brown, golden brown, yellow, brown-red and all colors of the fall months. Virgo is the mutable sign and Mercury rules during Wednesday. Countries under this sign are Greece, Turkey, Brazil, Mexico, Switzerland.

Organs under Virgo's or Mercury's rulership are small intestine, spleen, and pancreas. This is also the symbol for the complete health of the body because Virgo controls our metabolic processes.

Virgo is known as the excellent worker, someone who serves others, a person with tremendous analytical abilities, sometimes neat picky, but with good intentions. They tend to become excellent doctors, lawyers, writers, administrative workers, thriving in all these professions, which are demanding precise and timely data.

Virgos will have stable marriages, but only after they go through a crisis of adjusting to their partner, and they, above all other signs, can be too demanding in the terms of clean, scheduled and precise living conditions. Little Virgo children should be involved with education, especially natural sciences because their minds will very quickly awake and they will take control over their future if directed properly from an early age.

The Sun in Virgo or placed in the sixth house of the horoscope demonstrates a darker type or person, someone slim and not very tall. This position of the Sun shows the natural ability for serving others or generally being of service toward anyone or anything in life. Great doctors are born in this sign, as well as nurses, natural healers, and nutritionists. This is also auspicious for administrative works, extended writing, editing or checking and rechecking. What has been sowed in the springtime, time of Aries and Taurus, now is reaped. This is the period of the year where we take the look back at the agricultural results and make necessary calculations for the future.

The Moon in the sign of Virgo or placed in the sixth area of the chart describes the person with the sensitive stomach, many minor illnesses, bloating, but this placement also indicates working with women, in the female environment or frequent contacts with many people. This is an excellent position for taking care of babies or elderly people. Women or a motherly figure in the native's life can also behave like a small enemy. This is someone who is a good psychologist or a social worker.

Mercury in the sign of the Virgin shows an excellent writer, editor, someone who will very thoroughly control and correct other people's papers or words. This is also someone who is magnificently talented for the healing of any sort, but especially natural methods. This person uses the wide knowledge regarding herbs, light exercises like yoga or qigong, homeopathy, nutrition and those methodologies the native had tried on him/herself first, because of the earlier digestive disputes. Food heals everything, a person might often claim, with the same passion and fire as one Leo claims that the Sun cures everything. On the negative side of the Virgin, this Mercury is prone to exhausting verbal fights, talks too much in general and annoys children or children are annoying to this native.

Venus in Virgo or positioned in the sixth house of the chart is the worst place for this essence of pleasure. Venus is in the sign of its fall here in the astrological sense. Too much analyzing, too much realism, work is hard and people are looking at the soil, crops and fruit trees, not noticing how beautiful this Venus is. She also grows in poverty here and she has to find a way out, trough calculations related to the perfect choice for marriage, or through using her beauty, body or clever mind to secure her future, but those details will mainly depend upon other planetary aspects too.

Mars placed in the sixth house of the sign of the Virgin is the clear sign of digestive or serious inflammatory problems with the gut. And diabetes belongs to this category. A person is usually allergic to grains and from the grains, all other health problems arise. But at this place, Mars also indicates the elevated levels of stress, working in the aggressive kind of environment, meeting many furious younger men and dealing with them. The native also has a very analytical type of reasoning and this person is really diligent. This is a great position for scientific or medical research, planning and designing machinery or real-estate blueprints.

Jupiter is in the sign of his detriment in the sign of Virgo or generally speaking, this great teacher feels badly placed in the sixth house which deals with daily obligations and usually non-important matters when the sea of knowledge is waiting to be found somewhere far. This is the avatar that is standing on the edge of the farmer's market trying to sell eggs or vegetables. He will surely have some hard times to finish this task because in that particular place people are less interested in his insights about the perfect cosmic shapes of the egg or the structure of energy inside one apple. Jupiter feels here very restricted and misunderstood. This position also indicates gaining fats around the waist area. This is good for using the scientific agricultural method on the large properties.

Saturn placed in the sign of the Virgin and especially in the sixth house describes annoying chronic diseases and this might be the punishment for the native for not becoming a doctor because greatest diagnostics are born with their Saturn in Virgo. This is the case when the mind goes very deep searching and finding the real cause of any disease. This can also be the indication for gallbladder stones or very slow and sensitive digestion. This Saturn points to the poor ancestors who probably had to cope with the hunger and oppression to survive. On the positive side, this is the extremely good position if the native is in the industry of dried foods, like dried fruits and vegetables. Good for storing and selling grains, nuts, and seeds, also for the "dry" foods like biscuits.

Uranus in Virgo or placed in the sixth house can describe the sudden problems with pancreas, diabetes, strange sensitivity of the gut caused by electricity or any form of EMF waves, causing danger with some modern types of diagnostics, like the ultrasound. On the positive side, this is the image of the excellent radiologist or, generally, a doctor who deals with latest diagnostic machinery. This is also the symbol for the sudden destruction of crops caused by lighting and storms, and very serious viral infections going on in the guts.

Neptune in the sign of Virgin is the archaic symbol for the holy smoke. This is the clear inclination toward smoking tobacco or any other herb, especially those with hallucinogenic traits. This is a very dangerous placement for people who are prone to food poisoning, extremely toxic mushrooms, and all chemicals used for food preservation or for the purposes of the modern agriculture. This is the sign of unclear bacterial infection of the guts and of the crops in the field too. On the positive side, this Neptune placed in the sixth house can give talent for imagination and excellent storytelling if supported by other planets.

Pluto placed in the sign of Virgo or positioned in the sixth house if in major aspects with the other important celestial bodies, can point in the direction of discovering hidden or, most likely, buried treasure on the family's property. This can also be the sign that the native can suddenly realize that some ancestral heritage can be used in marvelous ways, while on the negative side this is a tumor or a bullet in the stomach, horrible or magnificent health depending on other aspects.

# LIBRA

The Sun transits through the sign of Libra from the 23rd of September until the 23rd of October and during this period of time, the Sun is about relationships, justice, and balance. This is the symbol for the business or marital partnerships, always focused on harmony.

The sign of Libra or the seventh house is all about dealing with others, being just, accomplishing the balance and success of both or all parties. The ruler of this sign is the planet Venus, which is here diurnal (during the day) according to a Ptolemy's Table of Essential Dignities. This is the male sign, the element is the air and the colors are green, light blue, turquoise, all gentle colors. Libra is the cardinal sign and Venus rules during Friday. Countries under this sign are Austria, Argentina, Tibet, Canada, Saudi Arabia.

Organs under Libra's or Venus's rulership are: kidneys and they are in the direct relations with the head (sign of Aries) in regards to controlling the blood pressure. This is also the symbolic sign describing how we function in the outer world receiving and answering to outer conditions.

Libra is the most famous sign of the beauty ideals, harmony between people and ideas of justice. However, on the negative side, this sign is full of snobbism, shallow behavior and pretending. Natives can be nice on the surface, but deep down in their souls, they are full of insecurities and therefore need established sets of rules. Generally, Librans are afraid of loneliness and when desperate they will commit to anyone willing to be with them. If the marriage starts earlier in life, it will usually break, but the later or the second marriage will last forever. Children of this sign should be thought to be independent and with a strong will, capable of making and sticking to their own decisions.

The Sun in the sign of Libra is in its fall. In other words, this in the worst possible place for the Sun. This means that the will of the person is weak because it is directed toward others. In this time of the year, everything is preparing to die or to sleep, harvest season is ending, and the whole nature is calming down. In ancient religions, this time was considered as the true beginning of the year because "And there was evening and there was morning, the first day" Bible, Book of Genesis, 1:3-5, everything begins from the dark, even before its conception, while being just the idea. Doing for others and having in mind their needs first is the death of the ego, therefore death for the Sun.

The Moon in the sign of Libra or in the seventh house is not such a good position either. Not so bad, like this is the case with the Sun, but still not very useful because the mind of the person is driven by emotions and those emotions are often scattered all around trying to be everywhere in every moment being present for everyone. This is hardly possible and many of the natives with this position of the Moon are considered to be shallow in their emotions. On the other side, this is the image of someone who lives for and through the social admiration. All of those fantasy or fake lives shown on social media platforms are the mirror reflection of this Libra's Moon. Positively speaking, a person needs to be close to someone through committed love or a business partner to be able to feel full and useful. In some cases, this is the indication of volatility in marriage or multiple marriages in the life of this person.

Mercury in the seventh house or in the sign of Scales is the clear image of the great lawyer, public speaker, someone who loves to show his words, speech or ideas in public. This is also the indication for the talented actor capable of memorizing huge amounts of dialogs. Excellent entrepreneur, even better negotiator. On the negative side, this person can be tricky and if Mercury receives negative aspects, this will show grandeur liar or deceiver. In any case, the native's children will be well raised and with good manners.

Venus in the sign of Libra or positioned in the seventh house is in its own home. However, this Venus is focused on relationships, instead of just material possessions. These possessions, in fact, in the kingdom of Libra are in the realm of spiritual, being airy in nature. These are all about beauty, balance, harmony, proper measure, proper manners, and the ability for lovely social communication. Great for partnerships of any kind. This Venus has slim, fairy body, lighter eyes or hair with delicate and beautiful moves, which are not so erotic in their nature, but more prone to elegancy.

Mars in the sign of Libra or positioned in the seventh house is in his sign of detriment. This Mars doesn't feel so good in the circle of women, in the ceremonial type of situations or mannered conversation. Especially in the seventh house, it can indicate frequent marital disputes and even a divorce. A person usually knows what is right and what is wrong in the relationship, but their partner simply can't adjust to harmonious life together and this is the source of all troubles. On the positive side, this is one very strategically oriented Mars. Ancient martial arts are based on this position due to the fact that they all have a foundation in the idea of harmony. The game of chess also belongs to this category.

Jupiter in the sign of Libra or placed in the seventh house of the chart describes the person who has good abilities when it comes to aesthetics, someone who is loved and respected in society and, most likely, someone who is very popular and can easily spread ideas in certain social circles. This is also the respected actor or performer of any kind of art. The person with this position tends to rise in society after marriage, but it can be good for business partnerships too. If afflicted this planet gives some sort of religious disputes with the spouse or even troubles in society regarding personal religious or spiritual views.

Saturn in the sign of Scales exalts in that particular place, and this is also the case when it's in the seventh house. A person might wait a bit longer to get married, but once this marriage happens, it will be unbreakable. Saturn is all about duty and justice, and in the sign of Libra, this planet can show all of his power amongst other people surrounding the native with this position. It's pretty easy to be the best one and stand alone on the top of the mountain of success, which is the case with Saturn in Capricorn. However, it's far more demanding to be fair, focused and balanced when the baby is crying, the husband needs his dinner, while your mother is on the phone asking did you call her dentist, for instance. This is the excellent example of being in balance and with the stable mind when everything around you is crashing down. This is the real and the most powerful emanation of the planet Saturn. In relation to this is the story about the piece of coal, which had to go through extreme temperatures and pressures to become the diamond.

Uranus in Libra or placed in the seventh house is always about the partnership disruptions, divorces or marrying divorced person. These are fast and unstable partnerships, even in the business sense.

Neptune in Libra or especially when this planet is positioned in the seventh house indicates something unclear regarding marriage. In the best case scenario, a person will marry someone with eye problems or someone involved in film or TV acting. In all other cases, this could be the sign of lying or cheating in marriage and in business.

Pluto in the sign of Libra or when it's forming significant aspects with the other planets from the seventh house tends to behave in the brutal sense to the public. If the aspects Pluto makes are negative, this is someone who is hated by everyone, and popular due to this fact. It can also be related to a fated love stories or complete withdrawal from others.

# SCORPIO

The Sun transits through the sign of Libra from the 23rd of October until the 22nd of November and during this period of time the Sun is about death, depths, and resurrection. This is the symbol for the transformation, sexual energy, as well as unearned incomes.

The sign of Scorpio or the eighth house is all about transforming the ideas, body, diving deep into the world of the occult or unknown. The ruler of this sign is the planet Mars, which is here nocturnal (during the night) according to Ptolemy's Table of Essential Dignities. This is the female sign, the element is the water and the colors are black, of course, burgundy red and purple. Scorpio is the fixed sign and Mars rules during Tuesday. After its discovery, planet Pluto is generally considered to be the co-ruler of this sign together with Mars. Countries under this sign are Turkey, Panama, Lebanon, Cambodia, Angola.

Organs under Scorpio's rulership are: the genitals and all excretion organs. This is also the symbolic sign describing how the life is transformed in us through the energy of passion, creating a new being, and also what we need to let go of to become free.

This is the sign of the "other side". The person had to go through some harsh experience in life, perhaps even more of those experiences to become initiated into the real Scorpion. This is the special sign because its transformations are always going through three phases. First, the native is a Scorpio, low, furious and bad. Then it becomes the Eagle, above everyone else, but vengeful. And the third stage is when the native becomes the Phoenix or the Dragon, which depends on the astrological tradition of a certain area. In this phase, a person is higher than anyone else, but it can also transform lives and this time in a powerful and positive way.

The Sun in the sign of Scorpio or placed in the eighth house of the chart is all about very dramatic transformations throughout the whole life. This Sun already died in the sign of Libra, so now it's wandering through the underworld seeking for the purpose and the meaning, not just of life, but of death itself. The will is here focused, magnetic, dramatic and it searches for the way to make a breakthrough. This Sun doesn't fear responsibility or risk, it can't and it won't stop in its pursuits, no matter whether the native with this position of the Sun achieves something or just watches.

The Moon in the sign of Scorpio or in the eighth house is in the sign of its fall, the worst place for sensitive Moon, indeed. The soul is forced to dive deep into the unknown and usually, the native with this position is forced to go through some serious problems from an early age. This person was hurt in a very horrible way due to disputes with the mother or any motherly figure around. He/she was emotionally abandoned and ridiculed by the ones this person needed the most, or in some cases, the mother couldn't protect the child because she had to go through tremendous pain. The second phase this Moon has to go through is self-hatred and hatred toward members of the family, tribe or anyone involved with a challenging experience. The Moon like this is capable of thinking and conducting any type of revenge and even black magic rituals. And the third step toward transformation is forgiveness. This Moon understands and forgives for all the troubles it had to experience and in those moments, it gains supernatural powers to heal others. This is a great placement for energy healers, exquisite doctors, pharmacists or chemists.

Mercury positioned in the eighth house or in the sign of Scorpio is the clear indication for someone who is talented in occult sciences or with the gift of clairvoyance. This is great for astrologers, tarot card readers and similar professions. At the same time, this is the excellent position for diagnostics in medicine, but the native might have a dirty or simply rude way of speaking.

Venus in the sign of Scorpio or placed in the eighth house is in its sign of detriment. The queen of pleasure is lost in the darkness and here she has nowhere to turn but directly to the king of the underworld. She is prone to sexuality, her beauty can become cheap or aggressive depending on the other planetary positions and she thrives through challenging or lost romances. The person with this position of the planet Venus had his/her heart broken many times and love can even be found through some very tragic events. Although mainly considered as cheap, this Venus can be an exclusive type of a woman who went through all sorts of dramatic events in her life and now became excellent in the skills of war and strategic thinking. She is the type of a perfect female warrior which is used in the battle when all other options have failed. And consequently, she is the queen in the game of chess who will be sacrificed for victory. A woman with this mission is the highest symbol for this Venus.

Mars in Scorpio is in his own kingdom, but with some slight differences than in his other house – Aries. Here this planet is in his night mode, so we no longer deal with that naïve and open-minded type of Mars. This planet in Scorpio is known as the excellent strategist, he is something like the war advisor for the Sun and his opinion, targets, and goals are always hidden. Mars is the warrior who is skilled and extremely precise with weapons, but unlike the Aries Mars who loves to join forces with others, this one thrives when he works alone. This is the image of the hitman, the sniper or someone who waits in the dark corner of the street with a knife. In the medical sense, this is the perfect position for the best surgeons, but if this is not the case, then the native falls ill in a sudden manner and most of those illnesses are acute, hard, but short lasting. These are commonly inflammations of the sexual organs or bladder.

Jupiter placed in Scorpio or in the eighth house of the chart can lead a person toward such extensive and positive transformations that this person can become much more skilled, better or far in front of everyone else in life. If negatively aspected, in this case, Jupiter will direct such a person toward a leading position, but in a shameful business, like running a mafia or dangerous religious cult. This position also indicates great returns on investments or a marriage with a person who makes a significant income.

Saturn placed in the eighth house of the horoscope or in the sign of Scorpio describes a long life, but usually with long chronic illnesses too. The person might have problems with kidney stones or sand and something is always wrong with the sexual drive or large intestine. On the positive side, this is good for investing in precious metals and stones, and also properties, especially old and valuable ones.

Uranus in Scorpio or in the eighth house can be very dangerous because Uranus is considered to be the higher octave of the planet Mercury. This Uranus can indicate sexual perversion, harsh character or sudden death caused by electricity. The energy created in this area of the chart is too strong, and it causes disruptions and eruptions.

Neptune in the sign of Scorpio or placed in the eighth house points to the danger of drowning. Besides this, a person is in the constant danger of infection through water, bathing or sexual contacts. This is also a love of drugs, legal or illegal and if other aspects are supportive in a negative or positive way, this person can become a drug dealer or a pharmacist

Pluto placed in Scorpio or in the eighth house can be very peaceful if it's not in aspect with the other planets or triggered by their transits. If this Pluto is active in the chart, then this can be the sign of a great healer, but it can also point to the direction of a murderer, deadly explosions, fires, military graveyards and all things related to the symbolism of joined Mars and Pluto, which means fear, terror, and trauma.

# SAGITTARIUS

The Sun transits through the sign of Sagittarius from the 22nd of November until the 21st of December and during this period of time the Sun is about discoveries, higher learning, and expansion. This is the symbol of the spirituality, joy of newness trough intellectual and physical activity.

The sign of Sagittarius or the ninth house is all about reaching for the higher ground and exploring the depthless quality of the human or a godly soul. The ruler of this sign is the planet Jupiter, which is here diurnal (during the day) according to Ptolemy's Table of Essential Dignities. This is the male sign, the element is fire and the colors are golden yellow and saffron orange. Sagittarius is the mutable sign and Jupiter rules during Thursday. Countries under this sign are Australia, Spain, China, South Africa, Kenya.

Organs under Sagittarius' rulership are the liver, buttocks, and thighs. This is also the symbolic sign describing how freedom is achieved after the drama coming from Scorpio, where we keep out the inner fire and how to reach it.

The sign of the Archer values his freedom the most and therefore earlier marriages usually end through divorce. Second marriage might be with the person with the greater age or cultural difference when most of the Sagittarians search for novelty and liberty is already satisfied. Children of this sign should be thought to respect social norms, but to spend most of their time outside pursuing sports and pieces of evidence in the field of natural sciences. The broadness of the mind or the human soul are their highest aims, so don't limit them and they will show their best.

Sun in the sign of Sagittarius or placed in the ninth house of the horoscope clearly describes the person who is prone to becoming a great teacher, the real guru for younger generations. This is also someone who loves to travel to distant places and delights through the ideas of constant growth and research. A person like this is always talented for comedy and even in the midst of very hard or demanding events, this person finds the way to lighten everyone around them. Physically this is the portrait of someone with a big or at least tall body, but if afflicted this Sun will show someone who is short and fat.

The Moon in the sign of Sagittarius or positioned in the ninth house is someone who is restless when it comes to traveling. This person will change many places and his home will be on the road. Later on in life, the native can settle through marriage, but most likely with the person who originates from completely different religious or cultural background. On this place, the soul is seeking for better answers than the ones which were given just through the official process of education. The mother figure is prominent in the native's life as someone who is truly educated, but at the same time bighearted and open-minded.

Mercury in the sign of Sagittarius is not in its best position because this is the sign of its detriment. And the same applies for the Mercury in the ninth house. The mind of the person is down to earth here where it's supposed to fly higher. It's like someone let the supermarket cashier into the university laboratory to supervise experiments, or it can look like the gathering of the traders in the temple. The person with this position lacks a deeper understanding of life and therefore shows as inadequate for the situations he/she has to go through. On the positive side, this is the image of the person who works on the supportive and administrative types of jobs for universities or spiritual organizations.

Venus placed in the sign of Sagittarius or placed in the ninth house of the horoscope is an indication that this person, or a woman, or a female energy in a native, will just love to travel to exotic destinations. A woman like this doesn't seek luxury and comfort; she delights in oriental scents, customs, and patterns. Her clothes can be sloppy, but colorful and she just loves the hippy style. Her desires are broad and related to erotica, not so much real passion. And she will never forget to show her long legs or talk about her Ph.D. Giving her the freedom to speak her mind and to move wherever she wants will be the best way to attach her to yourself.

Mars positioned in the ninth house or in the sign of Sagittarius is known for his good mood in any situation. This is truly strong, but at the same time, this is a peaceful Mars which uses his strength for some higher purposes than just fighting. These are the people who love horse riding, hunting, tennis, car races, tennis, archery, all those sports or activities which will move the person further, but at the same time indicate the certain dose of nobility. This type of Mars won't get provoked so easily, he will rather think about the whole situation with humor and probably decide to walk away from an excessive situation. This is the great position for archaeologists, travel guides, sports instructors and also doing business related to spiritual or religious themes or working with foreigners.

Jupiter in the sign of Sagittarius or placed in the ninth house can ensure magnificent success in philosophy and any natural sciences. This is someone who is generous, righteous and good-hearted, but at the same time, this is a person who is internally free and besides this, also has significant social and financial successes. This success is ensured in his plans, speculations or any type of endeavor too. Good positions for this native are a lawyer, judge, priest, organizer of others, but mostly in the field of spirituality. In good aspects, this person is noble with high moral standards and influence on others, while with affected Jupiter, this shows like someone who exaggerates in everything and this can lead him to failure in life and completely ruin his reputation.

Saturn in the sign of Sagittarius or placed in the ninth house of the chart is the portrait of a serious deep thinker and someone successful regarding metaphysical issues. This can also be an indicator for a great astronomer if other aspects are supporting. In usual cases, this is the sign of someone who wants to pursue higher education in the form of the university diploma, but due to circumstances the person can't achieve this, mainly due to the necessity of daily working tasks needed for financial survival. This is also the symbol for refugees, walls, obstacles trying to reach better living conditions, problems with authorities and issues with legal matters.

Uranus placed in the ninth house or in the sign of Sagittarius can pull the person toward spiritual disruptions in some sense. A person usually seeks to run away from national or family religious traditions and in this search finds many new teachings which are not appropriate or leave this person disappointed. If positioned well through aspects with other celestial bodies in the chart, this is the portrait of someone who is talented for incorporating the latest technology into traditional ways of learning, and also someone talented for astronomy, astrology and maintaining frequent contacts with technologically savvy foreign people.

Neptune in the sign of Sagittarius or positioned in the ninth house of the chart is someone who dreams about distant exotic places and those dreams are filled with fantasies of peace, meditation, rest, relaxing. In a good position, this person visits temples, especially monasteries where spiritual knowledge is delivered through wise and often foreign persons. In negative aspects, this is someone who can suffer from asthma, there is also the possibility of breathing problems related to hiking or alpinism, or generally speaking, problems with religious beliefs covered with illusions or inhaling illegal or harmful substances.

Pluto in the ninth house or placed in the sign of Archer is all about phantasm, ideological movements, and turnarounds which ruin cultural monuments, irrational philosophical systems planned for the future, using force to reach freedom, using pray to heal, complete transformation through religion.

# CAPRICORN

The Sun transits through the sign of Capricorn from the 21st of December until the 20th of January and during this period of time the Sun is about hierarchy, structure, and power. This is the symbol for the established position, hard work, and dedication.

The sign of Capricorn or the tenth house is all about reaching the top of the mountain, corporate ladder, or any other type of reputation we project into the outer world. The ruler of this sign is the planet Saturn, which is here nocturnal (during the night) according to Ptolemy's Table of Essential Dignities. This is the female sign, the element is the earth and the colors are black, coal shades of gray and sometimes brown. Capricorn is the cardinal sign and Saturn rules during Saturday. Countries under this sign are Great Britain, India, Mexico, Sudan, Bulgaria.

Organs under Capricorn's rulership are bones in general, knees and teeth. This is also the symbolic sign describing how the position and reputation are fought for, established and maintained through constant hard work and focused efforts.

This is the sign of the strong family or national tradition. Through struggle, oppression and hard environmental conditions, the native will sharpen his/her skills and become very powerful, seeking for the better or the best of life. Capricorn is the sign of the true material wealth and people born like Goats will ensure their lives with the best lands, real-estates, and piles of gold. They tend to get married a little later in life, but those marriages are stable as rocks and their partners know what is expected of them right from the start. Children are shy and they should be encouraged to enjoy life more and to try to be more empathetic toward others.

The Sun in the sign of Capricorn or placed in the tenth house of the chart indicates the person who is goal oriented, has respectful and highly established fatherly figure in his/her life and seeks to repeat his father's success or usually do better. This person might feel lonely and isolated in the earlier ages, but in the second part of life, the native suddenly awakens, focuses and achieves success through dedication. The Sun doesn't feel particularly good in this sign; however, this Sun is absolutely certain that it can't get a position or gain possessions solely through the ego, but through using all sorts of interactions with others, positive as well as negative. Strong, but controlled and guided will is fully operational.

The Moon in the sign of Capricorn or placed in the tenth house is in the sign of its detriment. The Moon simply doesn't feel good in the cold and rough environment. Perhaps it can be good for a father's type of energy, but it surely doesn't suit the soul of the mother. This can be the indication that relationship with the mother was rather cold or she was unavailable for the native during the phase of childhood in some sense. Feelings are frozen or very slow in expression. This doesn't mean that this person is senseless in any way, but he/she is closed, conservative and afraid because the outer world is oppressive and even brutal.

Mercury in the sign of the Goat or placed in the tenth house points to someone who is slow, but meticulous during childhood years, probably with speech problems, and this person can even seem to be not so bright for people surrounding him/her. However, in the more mature phases of life, this Mercury starts to catch the general rules of life, especially business and becomes a very shrewd businessman. This is the great entrepreneurial spirit, someone capable of running multiple businesses at once.

Venus in the sign of Capricorn or placed in the tenth house is the portrait of a lady, simply put. In the second part of life, this Venus starts to show her beauty and magnificent sense of elegance. These are usually wives of powerful business and political figures, neatly dressed and with the excellent manners. When her hair becomes gray, she reaches the peak of her power. If she gets acquainted with the business or corporate world, then success can be found through female types of industries, like fashion, accessories, and cosmetics. Love is found through the area of work and in many cases, there is the age difference greater than seven years between marriage partners.

Mars in the sign of Capricorn or placed in the tenth house of the chart is a phenomenally good place for this Mars because this is the sign of his exaltation. This planet becomes the strongest here, not just in the terms of his physical power, but this is included also. He is at his peak because he has the focused mind and his will is made of steel. In most cases, he came from a very poor environment and he had to fight for everything in life. He is accustomed to hunger and to lacking the basic means in life. So, he fights and learns along his path. In the physical sense, this is one very naturally strong Mars because he didn't build his muscles spending time in the gym, but through physical work, which made him capable of wrestling with a bear, any bear in life. In the terms of a career, this position is great for real-estate business, construction building, and engineering, dealing with metallurgy or any highly developed industry.

Jupiter placed in the sign of Capricorn or in the tenth house of the horoscope is someone who achieved success in the public life, but through a long process or proving his/her skills or expertise. This process most likely came with the help of foreigners or priests and it seemed to everyone else that it was accomplished with the godly peace or in a noble manner. This is also the portrait of the supreme judge in the state, the highest priest or the best public speaker or a guru. The native can climb very high regarding careers, which are dealing with education, especially related to the business kinds of education. However, Jupiter is in its fall here and he always feels limited by circumstances.

Saturn placed in his home sign, the sign of Capricorn or in the tenth house speaks volumes about the long and hard pursuit for security, expertise and recognition. This is someone who grew old trying to create his/her kingdom and now stands on the top of the world or on the top of the mountain. Saturn placed here is all about tradition, crypts, old castles with dungeons and dragons underneath. These are all servants, slaves and poor oppressed people. This is the sign of someone who loves to eat simple peasant food, goat's meat, burnt a bit, with dried foods also. If in positive aspects this is the indication for the rich and powerful person, not necessarily famous or loved by everyone. This is the symbol for properties, lands, wealth in the big sense of this world. Industries related to this position are mining, archeology, metallurgy, machinery and similar hard, but at the same time very profitable jobs.

Uranus in the sign of Capricorn or placed in the tenth house of the chart describes a very unusual career for the native. This can be the sign of someone who applies very advanced technologies and mixes them with traditional methods. Astronauts, IT engineers, inventors and many more fall into this category. In negative aspects, this is someone who changes careers frequently, doesn't get along with authorities and therefore pursues a unique type of career and recognition.

Neptune in the sign of the Goat or placed in the tenth house can indicate someone who is involved in the shady businesses or politics, but in very problematic ways which frequently include lies. If this planet is receiving positive aspects in the chart, then it indicates great success in the chemical, agro-chemical, pharmaceutical or oil industry and the person with this position can rise above everyone else if the planet Saturn is positioned well also.

Planet Pluto placed in the sign of Capricorn or in the tenth house can be the sign of the remarkable career in all areas which deal with engineering, machinery, real-estate, properties in general, excavations, mining and highest levels of banking. On the negative side, this is the aggressive oppression, military power, war criminal, dangerous magic and cults, production of weapons, dogs of wars, nuclear power plants and weapons.

# AQUARIUS

The Sun transits through the sign of Aquarius from the 20th of January until the 18th of February and during this period of time, the Sun is about newness, equality, and diversity at the same time. This is the symbol for the technological and social advancement, as well as grouping of the people.

The sign of Aquarius or the eleventh house is all about being equal with others, uniting for the sake of the common cause and at the same time streaming for the higher ideal. The ruler of this sign is the planet Saturn, which is here diurnal (during the day) according to Ptolemy's Table of Essential Dignities. This is the male sign, the element is the air and the colors are light blue, silvery blue and washed out gray shades. Aquarius is the fixed sign and Saturn rules during Saturday. After its discovery, planet Uranus is considered to be the co-ruler together with Saturn. Countries under this sign are Russia, Iran, Syria, Sweden, Sri Lanka.

Organs under Aquarius' rulership are lower legs, complete neurology and lymphatic system. This is also the symbolic sign describing how our dreams can become the reality if we all unite, focus and work for mutual benefits.

Nothing is stable in this sign, especially marriages and relationships of any sort. People unite under one idea and then separate when conditions tend to change. Children are good hearted, but often without any manners and they should be thought to respect order a little bit more, and also they should be kept away from technological gadgets. But this is a lost battle in advance.

The Sun in the sign of Aquarius or placed in the eleventh house of the horoscope is its sign of fall here. This is the time of exhausting winter on the northern hemisphere and the Sun shows its face for a very short time during the day. At the same time, astrological interpretation points toward the sign of Leo where the Sun is in its home. Leo is the symbol for the ruler, the king, while Aquarius is the symbol for the people. And the Sun naturally doesn't feel supreme surrounded with those plain, raw and often rude souls. On the other side, the Sun placed here is all about the change and creating plans for the better future.

The Moon placed in the sign of Aquarius or in the eleventh area of the chart is describing someone who is prone to change and those emotional changes are highly dependent upon the changes going on the social circles of the native. A person with this position is interested and open toward anyone and any idea, but at the same time, the native lacks the deeper understanding how the life operates. Yes, it's not fair, the native often thinks and more often speaks, *why don't all rich people/corporations/countries just give up all money/properties/wealth to the poor and we will all be equal and happy*. At the same time, this person forgets about the hierarchy of power and the laws of evolution. There is not such a thing as being equal in this Universe and that is out of the reach or understanding of this Moon. On the positive side, it's easy to cheer up this person and the mother or the motherly figure was creative and joyous through this person's childhood.

Mercury placed in the sign of Aquarius or in the eleventh house could be, and in some rare cases is, the talent of the magnificent writer, if this person could manage to organize his/her mind and escape from shallow or daily disruptions. In all other cases, this is the real messenger and this person thrives in the careers related to IT technology, content writing, social media influence, journalism, trending and similar types of jobs which don't require deep understanding or proven and double checked information. If positioned negatively relative to other celestial bodies, this Mercury is capable to ruin its own reputation with rumors and gossips and hardly able to plan or to envision the future. The native just loves technological gadgets.

Venus placed in the eleventh house or in the sign of Aquarius is more about showing off in society than feeling the real pleasure inside. Love can be found in the places of mass gathering, like fairs, national celebrations, clubs, parties and of course, social media. In this particular horoscope house, love shouldn't be deep or dramatic; it's more about the leisure type and "look at me, look at us" representation. Erotica is present but without any real or lasting sexual passion. This Venus also thrives on sex exchanging games; she can be he, or even it, whatever that means in her/his/ its head. She loves to look different than the norm, but at the same time, she needs to be protected by the social circle which dresses or behaves in the same or similar manner.

Mars in the sign of Aquarius or placed in the eleventh house of the chart describes the person who is inclined generally in technology and engineering. These are all those guys who are prone to mechanical repairs related to cars, electricity, plumbing, construction building. This Mars is not the strongest and he is completely aware of this fact, but at the same time, he knows he can become unbeatable if he unites with others. If Mars receives negative aspects, then this can be the indication of a street gang membership, grouping for destruction causes. In positive aspects, this Mars unites with others to be able to make a breakthrough in technology, daily working tasks or exploring the unknown territories. Poor and oppressed groups of people who are seeking for their happiness elsewhere traveling long distances are the symbol for joined efforts of this type of masculine energy.

Jupiter in the sign of Aquarius or placed in the eleventh house is not in such perfect condition here, but this is far from being bad for the native's life. This person surrounds herself with a great number of other people and most of them are educated or at least influential in society. Networks of friends, business associates, valuable mentors, good social position, great plans for the future, these things are all covered and protected by the planet Jupiter in Aquarius. If in a positive aspect with Uranus, this can also indicate lottery winning or a sudden windfall of money. Also, Jupiter placed here can be the wonderful teacher for the masses and an excellent social worker. In negative aspects, the native has a distorted sense of spirituality and bad social position.

Saturn in the sign of Aquarius or placed in the eleventh house of horoscope is in his own house here, where this planet delights in the ideals of uniting the poor and turning against the established government or king or whoever is in charge. This is the symbol for washed out working uniforms, great movements of pioneers or refuges, hunger, but with the burning desire for a better future. At the same time, this points in the direction that person is surrounded with older or poor people, bounded by the same principles, beliefs, and prejudices.

Uranus in the sign of Aquarius or placed in the eleventh house of the horoscope speaks volumes about instability related to relationships or career. This is also someone who takes risky investments and in negative aspects, this is the person who is the blind follower of trends, easily changes his/her mind and the shallow thinker. In the positive aspects, this is the image of a great inventor, someone who stands out from all due to his/her unique way of thinking and living.

Neptune in the eleventh house or placed in the sign of Aquarius indicates someone who enjoys very foggy company. Something is not clear here when the friends are involved. They might be prone to illegal substances, actions or ideas. Good for electronic types of music or modern arts related to technology, bad for investments and planning.

Pluto in the eleventh house or placed in the sign of Aquarius, and if affected significantly by other planets, has the ability to turn friends into enemies. This could also be the member or the leader of the very dangerous closed type of organization, or this can be someone with clairvoyant or visionary ideas.

# PISCES

The Sun transits through the sign of Aquarius from the 18th of February until the 20th of March and during this period of time the Sun is about diving deep into the unknown cosmic sea, mysteries and hidden issues of creation. This is the symbol for spirituality, but in the personal and internal sense, isolation and seeking wisdom through silence.

The sign of Pisces or the twelfth house is all about being equal with the higher power, being alone in the sea of changes, diving into the self and at the same time diving into the divine. The ruler of this sign is the planet Jupiter, which is here nocturnal (during the night) according to Ptolemy's Table of Essential Dignities. This is the female sign, the element is the water and the colors are dark blue, silver, and all pearly shades. Pisces is the mutable sign and Jupiter rules during Thursday. After its discovery, planet Neptune is considered to be the co-ruler here together with Jupiter. Countries under this sign are Portugal, North Africa, Scandinavia, Namibia, Samoa.

Organs under Pisces' rulership are feet, blood, and complete circulatory system. This is also the symbolic sign describing our inner desires, fears, and readiness to explore the inner types of truths.

Pisceans are known as the best pharmacists, musicians, and spiritual leaders, although many of them can be perceived as confused and lost in this world. They usually tend to wait longer for the proper marital partner and the children born in this sign should be thought to be more social and realistic.

The Sun in the sign of Pisces or placed in the twelfth house of horoscope describes the person who is shy, patient and kind. This Sun doesn't use any of his entitled credits or special treatments. The native seems to have a very hard first third of life and finds success in reclusive types of professions. Basically, he seeks to help others and achieves this goal through the hospital or religious types of job, and often he can be seen as the lonely artist. In positive aspects, this native gets help or achieves success traveling and living overseas and in certain cases, he gets valuable help from highly educated foreigners.

The Moon in the sign of Pisces or placed in the twelfth house is the image of a person with very unclear feelings, lost in the sea of deep revelations and always changing. This person is highly sensitive, and there is something unusual in native's relationship with the mother. The mother could be absent, seriously ill or even dead if this position is negatively affected by other natal planets and person seeks to build his/her own ideal of motherly energy around this fact. The soul feels a deep loss and it always desires to come back home, wherever this spiritual and safe place is. If the mother is present, then she takes the role of a teacher, a real guru in the native's life and this education takes unusual forms, which can have extreme quality or be disastrous, depending on other aspects.

Mercury in the sign of Pisces or placed in the twelfth house is in his sign of fall and detriment here also. This planet is all about the transmission of information and especially verbal expression, and at this place, this can't be done. Words scatter, they lose their meaning and information is distorted. This is the place where a person shouldn't speak or write at all, where the mind and logic are drowned in the sea of wider knowledge than this Mercury will ever be able to understand. However, you can't prove this to the mercurial type of person. He/she will try in spite any advice to keep silent and make many mistakes along the way. This is also the sign of the danger of being robbed by a pickpocket, of being gossiped about and having some small, but very determined enemy.

Venus in the sign of Pisces or placed in the twelfth house of the horoscope is in her position of exaltation here. But don't get so excited too soon because this place is all about isolation and Venus can have the purest feelings and the best looks in Pisces and still stand alone. This is the greatest position for artistic pursuits, especially singing and poetry, not so good for marriage, because Venus is still in the sign which is the symbol of loneliness. She is lovely, romantic and delicate in her communication. Love can be found in all closed places, like hospitals, islands or distant foreign lands.

Mars in the sign of Pisces or in the twelfth house describes the introverted type of character. He is far from being weak in this weird place, but he is turned toward inner, deeper or higher breakthroughs, and he is simply not interested in the outer world. Good professions for this position are sailors, scientific researchers, all people who have to explore something away from the crowd and usual noise. If affected negatively, this native will have very powerful enemies, sudden and dangerous diseases and he could be even physically attacked in the dark. In positive aspects, this can be the military doctor or even a silent hero.

Jupiter placed in the sign of Pisces or in the twelfth house is in his own house here. This might mean some emotional or psychological instability, especially in the childhood, because native with this position simply feels that there is much more in life than just passing fancy and shining, but truly shallow objects, events or people. Later on, this person develops broader knowledge and starts to understand the magic of all realms of existence. This is a very auspicious position for people who aim for the highest types of university education, as well as people who are prone to become monks or priests. At the same time, this points in the direction of valuable help coming from the educated person or moving permanently very far, in most cases over the ocean. If affected, this Jupiter will describe a person who is lost in this world and ends up in the hospital or in the monastery.

Saturn in the sign of Fish or placed in the twelfth house is someone very emotionally close, prone to deep thinking and also prone to prolonged, chronic diseases. The person will surely have to deal with some hidden enemies and in most of the cases, those will be elderly and very powerful people. Many times this person will suffer from some serious trauma related to the people representing a religion of origin. If affected negatively by other aspects, this position could lead a native right to jail. In some cases, this might be working there as the guardian, manager or a doctor, but in extreme situations, this will mean imprisonment. Health is overall weak and the danger of blood clots is always present.

Uranus in the sign of Pisces or in the twelfth house portraits the person who delights around the ideas of how close is the end of the world, conspiracy theories and of course, extraterrestrial visitors. This is someone who is full of extraordinary and even fascinating ideas, but the real problem here is that this person lacks the focus or stable energy to make those ideas true. At the same time, this position can represent the danger of sudden and very challenging viral infections or attacks coming from a psychologically unstable person.

Neptune positioned in the twelfth house or in the sign of Pisces simply loves to reside here, because this is its home. Based on this place's inspiration, music, poetry or craziness can go sky high. In the sign of Aquarius Neptune loves pharmaceutical supplement, but here, this planet will go deep into natural types of healing, like herbalism or homeopathy. The person with this position feels the strong desire to run away from reality and in negative aspects, this could mean the danger of drowning or choking. Great for pharmacists, though.

Pluto in the sign of Pisces or in the twelfth house is the symbol for hard internal battle, guilt complex, ecstasy and powerful healings through the process of praying.

# TAROT CARDS:

# CHAPTER ONE: GETTING STARTED

## WHAT IS TAROT?

The tarot is a deck of seventy-eight cards, which are used for divination, for gaining insight and guidance on your current situation and your path in life. All of human life, perhaps even all of life, is contained within the images of the tarot. By learning to read the cards, you will gain knowledge of yourself, of your relationships with others, and of the bigger picture, the pattern of your life. Deep symbolism and many layers of knowledge are encoded in the images of the tarot, and by learning to read the cards, you learn to delve into these layers and the many ways they reflect our human experience.

As well as giving you the individual meanings of the cards, this book will show you the ways they fit together and the stories they tell. The tarot is a picture book, illustrating human life, our responses to the world and ways of acting in it, and this book will show you how to read it. The book of the tarot works on both an outer level, showing us the events and circumstances around us, and an inner level, reflecting back to us our emotions, hopes and fears and the way they affect our actions. Tarot is a language, told in images, universal symbolism and motifs, and this book will help you to become fluent in it.

The seventy-eight cards of the tarot deck are divided into two main sections, the Major Arcana or Greater Trumps and the Minor Arcana or Lesser Trumps. The Major Arcana can be seen as a psychological or spiritual journey towards greater understanding and fulfilment, of ourselves and of the world around us. There are twenty-two 'greater trumps", taking us on a journey through the great archetypes and energies which inform our lives, from the Fool with his leap into the unknown to the completion and success of the World. The Major Arcana cards show universal forces and life experiences which we may not be able to control, but which have a profound effect on us and the way we live our lives. They include figures such as the Empress and Emperor, representing the archetypal mother and the archetypal father, and heavenly bodies such as the Sun and the Moon

The fifty-six cards of the Minor Arcana are divided into four suits, usually known as Wands, Swords, Cups and Pentacles. They are similar to the spades, hearts, diamonds and clubs of a standard deck of playing cards. Each suit is related to a particular element, symbolising, in turn, a particular area of life. Wands are the suit of fire, symbolising creativity, passion and action, and Swords are linked to the element of Air, to logic, reason and communication. Cups are the suit of water, representing our feelings and imagination, and finally, the Pentacles bring it all into manifestation in the realm of earth, symbolising the material world, our work, home and resources.

Each suit contains fourteen cards, beginning with the Ace and going up to Ten. The number cards combine symbolism from numerology with the elemental attributions of the suits to describe the realities of our journey through life, our experiences of relationships and connections with other people, the work that we do and the place that we live, all of the choices that we make on a day to day basis.

The Court cards are the Page, Knight, Queen and King, and they represent personalities and ways that we use the elemental powers in our lives. They are a kind of tarot "family" showing our progression from youth to maturity and the different ways that we experience and act in the world as we grow.

## WHY DO WE READ THE CARDS, AND HOW DO THEY WORK?

Most people think of tarot cards as a way of telling the future, and that is one of the ways of using the cards. But it's important to remember that we all have free will. The cards do not determine our future, our decisions and choices do that. What the tarot cards can do is help us to make those decisions, to look at possible outcomes of choices we may make, and in this way guide us on our path. The cards reflect our inner as well as our outer experience, so that they may show you your feelings around a situation, or your hopes and dreams, just as clearly as they show the situation itself.

There are many misconceptions and superstitions surrounding the tarot, and many people are put off using the cards, or even going for a reading because they fear being told that something bad will happen to them. Whilst its true that the tarot sometimes doesn't pull any punches, and may tell you what you don't want to hear, it will also tell you what you can do about it. Nothing is set in stone and even if a situation is beyond our control, we usually have some degree of choice in how we react to it. Whilst the tarot is most well known as a tool for prediction, it is actually more often used as a tool for contemplation and reflection, for connecting to our inner selves. You will find that often, you already know what the tarot cards tell you, you just didn't know that you knew!

When people say that they are scared of the tarot or of what it might tell them, their fear is more likely a fear of being exposed, of having their inner feelings and experiences brought into the open. Not only does this make many people uncomfortable, but the fact that a deck of cards, mere images printed on paper, may do so, makes them even more uncomfortable. But we might say that this discomfort also shows us tarot's greatest strength, as an objective viewpoint on our lives. The cards seemingly fall at random, and yet their meanings connect deeply to our experience and show us the "truth" of our lives, as we are experiencing it at that moment. Some believe that there is some unseen force at work around us, ensuring that the cards we pull are exactly the ones we need to see right now, others that some hidden part of our mind influences us as we shuffle and lay out the cards. There are many ideas and explanations about why the tarot works, but most come back to the idea of synchronicity, or correspondences. Most of occult (the word "occult" simply means hidden knowledge) thought is based on the idea that there is a correspondence or link between something outside of ourselves, such as the tarot cards or the planets in astrology, and something within our psyche. They do not cause or affect each other, rather they are at work in parallel, so that by looking at the external manifestation of the force, for example in the image on a tarot card, we become aware of the corresponding energy at work within us. Occultists refer to this idea using the phrase "As above, so below" - as the energies play out above us in the universe, so they also play out within us. You may have already experienced "synchronicities" when events around you seem to reflect your emotions or what is happening within you. Using the tarot is a way of consciously inviting these synchronicities, understanding them and using them to live our best lives.

## THE HISTORY AND EVOLUTION OF THE TAROT

The tarot cards have their origins in fifteenth-century Italy, where they developed partly as a game (giving rise also to modern day playing cards) and partly as a kind of teaching aid showing medieval religious and social images, such as Strength, Temperance and Judgement. For years they were mainly used for the game of Tarocchi and for gambling, although they were sometimes also used for fortune telling. In the eighteenth century and nineteenth centuries, occultists (those who study hidden and esoteric knowledge) became aware of the tarot cards and their powerful images, and decided that there was more to these cards than met the eye. They linked them to the hidden knowledge of ancient Egypt, to the Jewish mystical tradition of the Kabbalah, and even to traditions of ceremonial magic. Nineteenth-century occultists, especially the members of the Order of the Golden Dawn in the late nineteenth century, worked with the cards and developed them into the images that we know today. Whilst they added extra layers of meaning and correspondences to other spiritual systems such as astrology, the basic structure of the deck has changed little since the artist Bonifacio Bembo painted the first deck for a wealthy Italian family, the Viscontis, in the middle of the fifteenth century.

Many of the decks most easily available today are based on the so-called Waite-Smith deck, developed by Arthur Waite (one of those Victorian occultists mentioned above) and illustrated by Pamela Colman Smith. It was first published in 1910 and has become the basis for most tarot decks published today.

The Waite-Smith deck was the first to use images on the Minor Arcana cards. The earlier Marseilles or European tradition (still popular and widely used today) has images on the Major Arcana cards and "pips" for the Minor Arcana – seven pentacles for the seven of pentacles, three swords for the Three of Swords, and so on. Many people find that having scenes painted on all the cards, including the Minor Arcana, makes them easier to read and remember, and this is especially useful when you are first learning the cards. However the Waite Smith version of the tarot is not as definitive as some would believe, and the earlier European tradition still has much to teach us. Over time, as you become more familiar with the cards, you will find the images and tradition which work best for you. This book uses mainly the Waite Smith images, simply because they are most commonly found and referred to in the world of tarot, whilst also drawing on other traditions and versions of the tarot images.

# CHOOSING A TAROT DECK

When we begin to work with tarot cards, we are making a choice to work on a symbolic level, which goes deeper than using our mind and intellect. From the many hundreds of different decks available today, the right deck for you is the one whose symbolism resonates deeply for you, the one which gives you a flash of recognition as soon as you see the cards. This may not be something you can articulate or communicate with others, but as you'll soon learn, there is much about the tarot that defies easy explanation, and herein lies its power.

A wide variety of decks are available, from the traditional to the modern, with themes drawing on different belief systems and traditions and on many aspects of popular culture. Whether your interest is fairies, tattoos or Buddhism, there's a tarot deck out there to suit you. When choosing a deck, listen to your intuition and choose the one with images you are drawn to, as you will get the most profound results that way. Working with the tarot means working with symbolic energies and images, so choosing a deck with images which reflect your worldview, or maybe even challenge your worldview, is likely to bring you the best results. There's no right or wrong way to choose a deck, as long as it speaks to you on some level, and has images that resonate with your life experience and the way you see the world.

You may also want to take into account practical considerations such as the shape and size of the cards, and how easy you find shuffling them. Even something as simple as the colour palette can evoke an emotional response, and an emotional response is what you want when choosing "your" deck.

Decks can be bought online as well as in "new age" shops and bookshops. New age shops often have a folder or file with sample cards from the different decks they have available so that you can look at the cards without having to open a sealed deck. Online, there are websites such as aeclectic.net and tarotgarden.com have lists and reviews of hundreds of decks, so you can do some research before you buy to be sure of getting the deck that's right for you. Some people believe that you must be gifted a tarot deck, but there is no reliable origin for this so-called tradition, which probably dates back to when tarot decks were difficult to find and knowing somebody who had one was really the only way to obtain one. Now they are widely available, we have more opportunities to find "our" deck and make that all-important personal connection with it.

Many tarot readers end up acquiring more than one tarot deck, and some have large collections. You may find that you work regularly with one or two decks, and have others simply because you like the images. Some decks work better for quick readings, others for deep personal explorations, still others for meditation and spiritual practice.

## LOOKING AFTER YOUR CARDS

So you've got your cards, now what? The first thing to note is some easy ways to look after them, as they tend to come in a cardboard box which can get worn very quickly when you are constantly taking the cards in and out of it. Again, there are many traditions, usually of quite a modern origin, about how you should look after your cards, and again, you shouldn't worry too much about them, but follow what feels right to you. Many people believe that tarot cards should be wrapped in silk because silk is a natural fibre and is seen as a good insulator against psychic energies. So silk protects your cards on both a physical and a spiritual level. Other natural fibres such as cotton are also good, and keeping your cards in a wooden box is also a popular way to protect them. Your cards are a sacred tool and should be treated as such – look after them and they will look after you!

Many people prefer not to let others touch their tarot deck, as it can muddy the psychic energies the cards carry. Again, this is a personal preference, and of course, there is a difference between letting your nearest and dearest occasionally look through your cards, and complete strangers rifling through them.

When reading for others, many readers ask the querent (the person receiving the reading) to shuffle the decks, to add their own energy to the reading. This is also optional of course, and there are other ways for your querent to add their energy to the reading, without actually touching the cards, For example, they could tell you when to stop shuffling, or indicate the cards they want to choose from the pile.

Whilst to an outsider the cards may simply be pieces of cardboard, you will soon begin to feel a connection to them and see them as something more than mere objects. They do pick up and carry psychic energies. This is nothing to be afraid of and simply the way the cards work, but cleansing them every once in a while, or after doing lots of readings, is useful and some even consider it necessary.

There are many ways to cleanse your cards, and most make use of natural energies to do so. You can leave them out overnight in the light of the full moon, or the bright light of the sun. Be aware if you're doing the latter that some cards can bend a little in heat or humidity, so don't leave them for too long. Some people use crystals such as clear quartz or amethyst laid on top of the deck. If you do this, cleanse the crystal afterwards by passing it through running water. Smudging, or passing through the smoke from incense or even a fire, is a popular way to cleanse tarot cards, and is very effective. Many people use sage, although this is a Native American tradition and has been so widely appropriated that white sage is now an endangered species. Try to use a herb from your own cultural tradition, or look up the magical correspondences of the herbs you have in your kitchen. Rosemary or lavender are good, as are sandalwood or frankincense. Its fine to try a few different methods of cleansing your cards, and see what works best for you, and for your deck.

# How to read the tarot cards

Studying and reading the tarot can be a life's work, but all you really need to get started is a deck of cards, your intuition (a kind of inner knowing everybody has which goes beyond the intellectual) and some basic card meanings, which this book will give you. To do a tarot reading, we shuffle the cards and lay them out in a particular order, known as a spread. Each position in a spread has a meaning. A popular and simple three card spread, for example, includes cards representing the past, present and future. We then interpret the cards according to their position, using meanings developed over centuries as well as our own intuition. Becoming a good tarot reader means learning to synthesise these three elements – the meaning of the individual card, its position in the spread and in relation to the other cards in the spread, and the intuitive meanings which may seem to come out of the blue as you gaze at the cards.

Anyone can read the tarot cards, you don't have to have psychic skills or lots of book learning. All you need is the ability to still and open your mind and respond to the images you see before you. This book will guide you through the basics of tarot card meanings and how to combine them in a reading. Whilst learning the meanings off by heart using a book such as this one is useful, ultimately the best way to learn to use tarot cards is simply that, to use them. Do readings for yourself, for your friends and family.

The first thing to do before doing a reading, or using your cards at all, is to shuffle them. This comes naturally to some people, but others find it challenging. If you are not confident of your shuffling skills, there are other methods of making sure the cards are properly mixed up. For example, you could simply lay them face down on the table in front of you, and push them gently with a circling motion, so that they spread out into a "pool". Once you have moved them sufficiently, you can gather them back up into a stack, or simply choose the cards from the pool.

Some readers turn some of the cards upside down when shuffling so that in a reading they are "reversed". This can change the way they are interpreted, as reversals are seen as the shadow side of the energy of the card. Reversed cards may ask you to pay extra attention to that message, or show where energy is blocked and not quite ready to come into conscious awareness. This can be helpful, but some people find it confusing and see the full range of meanings in the card when it is upright. Reversed cards are often seen as the "negative" version of the card meaning, and so some people see them as alarming. However, the reversed meaning of a challenging card, such as the Tower or some of the Swords cards, can actually lighten the energy and make it less challenging. Once again, its a personal choice to include reversals in your readings, and there is no right or wrong answer. However its best to be consistent, so decide whether or not you want to work with reversals and then stick to it.

## GETTING TO KNOW YOUR TAROT DECK – SOME SIMPLE

### EXERCISES

Whilst you will want to start doing readings as soon as you can, it's a good idea to spend some time getting to know your cards and trying out different ways of using them. This allows you to build up a personal connection to the cards, and gain a knowledge of the tarot that goes deeper than simple book learning.

An excellent way to begin learning is to pull a single card when you get up each morning and keep the image in mind as you go through your day. At the end of the day, look in the book to review the standard meaning of the card, and see if how it relates to your day. You will find that patterns emerge – lots of Swords cards when you are studying for an exam, or lots of Major Arcana cards when you are going through a big change in life.

Another good technique is close observation. Choose a card, at random or one that you'd like to know better, and simply spend several minutes looking at it closely. Note as many details as you can – colours, clothing, posture, facial expressions. Look at the layout of the picture, where everything is in relation to everything else. Look at the background, there are often details there that are easy to miss. When you have observed the picture for a while, you can take a metaphorical step back and consider the mood, the attitude of any people in the image, and what meaning these imply.

If you read lots of books on the tarot or talk to lots of tarot readers, you may find that there are sometimes apparently contradictory meanings for the same card. This is because there are so many layers of interpretation to each card, and a meaning that resonates for one reader may leave another cold. When you are starting out, there are several places you'll want to look to get a sense of the possible interpretations for a particular card. The "LWB" or Little White Book, which comes with the deck, usually gives brief meanings for that specific deck, and some tarot cards come with a full book covering the particular meanings used by the creators of that deck. Other books, such as this one, give an overview of the traditional meanings for a card, and you can use these with any deck. As you gain experience with the cards, you will also find that you intuitively "sense" meanings for specific cards, during readings or meditations, and these can come across quite strongly. Personal intuitive meanings are by their nature subjective, but some see them as more meaningful than traditional interpretations for exactly this reason. They may work in a specific situation, for example when reading for a querent who has a specific reaction to a particular card.

All of these layers of meaning can be confusing, and you may find yourself wondering which is the "right" meaning. The answer is all of them, or maybe none. Every interpretation is equally valid, and the ones which resonate with you will be the ones which are right for you. The only answer is to practice reading, for yourself and others, and you will begin to get a sense of which method of interpretation works best for you. Some people prefer to memorise traditional meanings and use them as a jumping off point, others rely purely on the images and symbolism on the cards, and what their intuition is telling them that day. As you gain experience with the cards, you will naturally find yourself working in a particular way and responding to the meanings which ring true for you and your querent. Even the most experienced tarot readers are constantly discovering something new in the cards. The meanings are not fixed, and that is another of the great gifts of tarot. You may even find that the way you interpret particular cards changes and evolves over time, and that's fine too.

# CHAPTER TWO: THE MAJOR ARCANA

## THE JOURNEY OF THE MAJOR ARCANA

The twenty-two cards of the Major Arcana tell a story, describing the journey of the Fool as he moves from innocence to experience, from youth to maturity, from ignorance to enlightenment. This is a psychological and spiritual journey, giving us not only a deeper awareness and understanding of our worldly concerns but also a connection to universal energies. This is not a journey which takes place on a uniquely linear plane - life goes in spirals, and we travel around the path many times in our lifetime. The spiritual wholeness of the final card, The World, leads straight back to the innocence of The Fool, which is generally seen as the beginning of the sequence, but also fits in at the end. The journey of the tarot works on both a macro and a micro level - it is the journey of a whole lifetime, from birth through youth, middle and old age to death, and also the multitudinous smaller journeys, spirals within an individual life.

The first Septenary, from the Magician to the Chariot, describes the journey to maturity. The Fool encounters the masculine and feminine energies of the archetypal Mother (the Empress) and Father (the Emperor) as well as the Magician and the High Priestess, who represent the spiritual aspects of the masculine and feminine. The Fool becomes aware that he is part of a cultural or religious tradition, meeting the Hierophant, who can help him to decide where s/he belongs. As he grows to maturity, he becomes aware of others

163

and may fall in love, learning to relate to others and make choices for himself. Finally, the Chariot represents worldly ambition, as the Fool gains the power to achieve his goals.

However, achieving our goals doesn't always feel as satisfying as we might have hoped. Sometimes we get all that we ever wanted and wonder why we are not happy. Sometimes we don't get anything we wanted and simply wonder why. We begin to question our assumptions and social conditioning, why we think the way we do, whether there is more to life than we've been led to believe. This is the journey of the Second Septenary, as the Fool begins to question his path in life and to seek a deeper level of meaning. He discovers their inner Strength and develops a sense of right and wrong (Justice). He begins to look inwards, as the Hermit, and to seek his own wisdom and path in life, as he gains in maturity and experience. He begins to understand that life's ups and downs are not always of our making, encountering the Wheel of Fortune, and at the same time meeting the paradox that we may have more control over life than we assume. He may retreat for a while, shift his perspective and even find his world turned upside down, becoming the Hanged Man. This change in worldview may lead to a time of endings, of letting go of past ways of acting and being, as in the Death card. We have to let go of the old, to make way for the more meaningful life that we seek. This new freedom is reflected in the following card, Temperance, which represents the renewed balance between consciousness and unconscious, and is one of the calmest and most harmonious cards in the major Arcana.

In the final Septenary the Fool looks beyond his individual growth, and begins to wrestle with universal energies, coming to a deeper level of awareness and therefore a more profound ability to create change. Encountering the Devil, he becomes aware of the ways that we give away our power, to other people or to our own expectations, and the Fool is challenged to take back that power. The Tower follows, a breaking down of inner and outer structures which may feel painful (especially if we resist it), but which clears the way for a greater understanding. The Star brings a time of calm - coming through the disruption of the Tower brings a sense of relief and a renewed sense of trust and faith in the universe. The worst may have happened, but we have not only survived but thrived. The Fool meets the dreamy energies of the Moon and may get sucked into that shadowy and uncertain realm, but the clarity of the Sun helps him to connect to his inner truth, and find ways to express it. The Judgement card symbolises this rebirth and ability to follow our highest calling, leading finally to the fulfilment and integration of the World. Of course, nothing in life is static, and the completion of the World card opens the way for the next chapter, bringing us back to the Fool at the beginning of his journey.

We may not encounter the cards in this linear sequence when we do readings (although sometimes we do, and  is always a sign that your path is unfolding as it should). However knowing the story and the journey we take means that when Major Arcana comes up in readings, we have a sense of where we are on our journey, and what the next lessons might be. We can keep the journey in mind as we consider each of the Major Arcana cards individually.

# Individual Card Meanings for the Major Arcana

## Cards

## *0 The Fool*

Keywords: Free spirit, a leap into the unknown, a new beginning, the unexpected

The Fool card shows a young person, standing on the edge of a cliff. He carries little baggage and ignores the dog, symbolising conscious awareness, who barks at his feet. The Fool is spontaneous and lives fully in the moment. His actions may seem like folly to others, but he has faith and trusts that all will comes right in the end. He is open to whatever gifts come his way and has no expectations, either good or bad. Indeed he is acting from his impulses, which may or may not prove to be right. The Fool moves towards change without knowing what kind of change it is or where he will end up, and this doesn't worry him. In fact, he welcomes the unknown, the excitement of a new journey with no particular destination in mine. The Fool is playful and open, not minding that this can also make him vulnerable or even foolhardy. The archetype of the Fool appears in many mythologies, as a trickster, reminding kings and heroes of their truth and not letting them get caught up in their own hubris. Sometimes, the apparently foolish are the only ones able to speak truth to the established powers. We also see the importance of the Fool when we note that he is the only one of the Trumps to have survived the transition to the modern deck of playing cards. Just like the Joker, the tarot Fool travels where he will through the pack of cards and doesn't follow any rules.

Reversed or shadow aspects of the Fool include a tendency to rush ahead without any awareness of the possible consequences. On the other hand, it may mean remaining in your comfort zone and refusing to try anything new or simply taking life too seriously, being cynical or pessimistic.

When the Fool comes up in a reading, a new adventure is about to begin. It's time to take a risk, to leap off the cliff often depicted in this card and trust that the path will be there to catch you. This is the card of following your bliss, of ignoring the expectations of others and doing what feels right for you. Listen to the cosmic messages of the universe and also to your own inner voice, then take a deep breath, and jump!

# 1 THE MAGICIAN

Keywords: Inner power, creativity, focus, attention, putting ideas into action

The Magician is a powerful figure, with the forces of the universe at his command, shown by the position of his arms. His right arm is held high to receive the energies of spirit, and his left hand points downwards, indicating that he brings those energies into everyday reality, and makes something tangible with them. His magic wand symbolises authority and confidence, the masculine or active energies we use to do our work in the world. On his table are the tools of the four suits of the Minor Arcana, showing his inner resources and talents. The Magician is single-minded and pure in his intentions and represents our ability to establish our priorities, focus on our goals and then take action to make them a reality. The Magician is both potential and experience and reminds us that when we act from a higher purpose, we connect to our highest self. He represents knowledge, learning and initiative, all bringing the potential for growth. Like the Fool, the Magician can be a trickster, and in early tarot decks, he was often shown as a conjurer or even a juggler. He is the archetype of the wizard, the wise magician who can change the world with his powers. In some decks, he is depicted as a shaman, who walks in the otherworld and brings its wisdom back to the mundane world.

Reversed or shadow aspects of the Magician can be trickery or deceit, acting from self-interest or for personal gain, and not respecting the needs of others. Using his power to dominate others or for selfish reasons results in the Magician losing his connection to the higher power which guides him. The shadow side of the trickster is the conman who cheats others for his own personal gain.

In a reading, the Magician tells you that you have what you need to make your dreams a reality. It's time to take action to realise your potential, to tap into your willpower and inner vitality. Have confidence in yourself and your abilities, and use the power of your conscious mind to achieve your goal. Concentrating on the project at hand, whilst also listening to the wisdom of your higher self, is the best way forwards.

## 2 THE HIGH PRIESTESS

Keywords: intuition, secret knowledge, deeper meaning, hidden self

The High Priestess is a mysterious figure, connected with dreams, intuition and the messages of the unconscious. She is the Magician's opposite, the power of the unconscious mind, the shadowy inner self and the power of receptivity and stillness. As the keeper of ancient and eternal wisdom, she represents knowledge and awareness of the mystery of life, as well as collective and personal memory. The black and white pillars often shown on either side of her throne symbolise light and dark, inner and outer, thought and feeling, all the dualities which we experience in our lives. Behind the curtain, she guards the mystery which brings them into balance. Her connection to the moon, shown in her headdress and also in the crescent moon at her feet, reminds us that life moves in cycles, the ebb and flow and that the quiet dark is just as important as the times of light and action. She is the archetype of deep feminine understanding, connected to wisdom goddesses such as Sophia and Isis, and she understands the deep power of the unconscious and of the underworld. A historical or legendary source for this card is the story of the woman who was once elected Pope (strictly against the rules of the Catholic Church), only being revealed as a woman when she gave birth during an Easter celebration, and until the eighteenth century, this card was called the Papess. The persistence of this story reflects the importance of the feminine archetype even in the male-dominated medieval Christian church and also reflects the meaning of the High Priestess as a mysterious figure whose full self must remain hidden.

Reversed or shadow aspects of the High Priestess can be an inability to connect to our dreams or listen to our intuition, thinking literally or superficially, and assuming that we already know everything. The reversed High Priestess might also indicate that we have been passive for too long, and need to take action to change our situation.

When she comes up in a reading, the High Priestess says that now is not the time for action. This is a time to go inwards, to listen to your intuition which is likely to be strong right now. There may be hidden potential or a new possibility about to come to light. This is a time when you can connect to the inner mysteries, to a sense of something greater than yourself.

## 3 THE EMPRESS

Keywords: fertility, creativity, generating new life, abundance, fruition, feminine energy

The Empress is the energy of the archetypal Mother, bringing new life to birth and embodying the fertility and abundance of nature. She is often shown as a pregnant or surrounded by the fruits of the harvest, showing the luxuriant energy of life and all its bounty. She speaks of creative abundance, of the fulfilment of our heart's desires, of the pleasures of the senses. Her sceptre of power is topped by a globe, reminding us that we create, literally bring into being, our own world. The Empress symbolises the passionate, even sensual approach to life, the power to give and take experience and emotions without limit or restriction. The stream often depicted at her feet symbolises both the unconscious, connecting her back to the High Priestess, and the waters of life, which ensure that everything grows and flourishes. She shows us how we can use our imagination and creativity to generate ideas and to birth them in reality. She also reminds us of the need to balance patience and action, to allow the harvest to develop in its own time so that it can grow to its full potential. The Empress represents synthesis and harmony, the unity which is born from the dualities of light and dark, action and receptivity. She is firmly rooted in our present experience and our connection to the world around us but also holds an awareness of our potential and what we are able to create.

Reversed or shadow aspects of the Empress may be struggling to connect with our emotions or ability to nurture ourselves and others, not giving others the space they need to be themselves, and sometimes destroying instead of creating. Reversed, the Empress might also suggest an over-abundance rather than a lack of emotions.

In a reading, she indicates a time of abundance, creativity and growth. You may be bringing a new project into being, nourishing and nurturing it into reality. It's a time to connect to nature and to the powers of your senses. She reminds us that abundance is not just about the material, but about gratitude for the many gifts life gives us each day. Take time to nourish whatever is most important to you, focusing your energy and attention on it.

## 4 THE EMPEROR

Keywords: authority, power, control, boundaries, masculine energy

The Emperor is the archetypal energy of the father, an authority figure who seeks to control and organise. He may represent social conformity, rules and regulations and the need to maintain order. He is confident in his right to rule and expects others to follow his lead. He is the master builder and the force of civilisation, bringing order to chaos and setting the rules which ensure that society functions successfully. He sets standards and social expectations and expects them to be met. The Emperor is a man of reason and logic, as well as action. He protects all those within his care, bringing security and comfort to his people. He has served his time on the battlefield and still wears his armour under his robes, ready to defend his people if he needs to. Now he represents the establishment and the social order, the father as guide, protector and provider. He is often seen as a very traditional, perhaps even old-fashioned, version of the father archetype as somebody rather remote and distant, who makes the rules and enforces discipline. A more positive approach is to see the Emperor as the creator of boundaries, helping us to know who we are as an individual and what our place is in the world. Most of us need to interact with mainstream society, to a greater or lesser extent, in order to live our daily lives, and we need to conform to certain behaviours to be accepted into that society, such as not harming others.

Reversed or shadow aspects of the Emperor include a tendency to control others, getting angry or defensive if our authority is challenged, becoming aggressive or dominating. On the other hand, the Emperor reversed can mean an inability to make decisions or take control of the situation.

In a reading, the Emperor asks you to look at your boundaries, and to your sense of inner authority. Are you in control of your life or are you trying to control those around you? It might be time to take on a leadership role, or to get clear about your direction and purpose in life. The Emperor indicates a need to take responsibility for yourself, to become the ruler of your own life. Getting organised and focused are also indicated by this card.

# 5 THE HIEROPHANT

Keywords: tradition, spiritual knowledge, teaching, education, group awareness

The Hierophant is a priest-like figure, usually shown with one or two acolytes or students who receive the knowledge and traditions he passes down. He symbolises established knowledge, the cultural and religious beliefs which inform our view of the world. His beliefs and ideas have been proven over time, which gives them authority and power but may also make them feel restrictive or rigid. The original name for this card was the Pope, linking it to the inner wisdom of the Papess or High Priestess, and this card can be seen as the outer manifestations of that wisdom, the church or belief systems which guide our society. However many people are now rejecting the established churches and choosing to follow their own spiritual path and ideally, the Hierophant is an inner teacher, the part of ourselves which seeks to understand the mysteries of the universe and the powers that guide us. He guides us through rituals and celebrations, the events which mark the rhythms of our lives and give them meaning. The Hierophant also represents groups and structures in society, the desire to conform and feel part of a group. This sense of belonging can bring security or restriction, and again as our inner guide, the Hierophant asks us to question our beliefs, not to mindlessly follow the ideas of others. We can draw on the wisdom of our traditions whilst also adapting it to work better in our own lives. Sometimes this card can refer to a giving away of responsibility, sticking to the rules in order to avoid thinking for ourselves about what is right and wrong.

Reversed or shadow aspects of the Hierophant may be intolerance of the beliefs of others, or blindly accepting other people's ideas, group or personal dogma. The Hierophant reversed can also suggest rebelling for the sake of it, rejecting the traditional or conventional but not replacing it with anything meaningful, or developing our own original ideas.

When the Hierophant comes up in a reading, you may be feeling drawn to a spiritual or religious tradition, or feeling the need to rebel against it and seek your own wisdom. You may be considering your group identity and wondering where you belong, or considering your beliefs and worldview, and how they inform your choices in life.

# 6 THE LOVERS

Keywords: relationship, love, inner and outer union, bringing together of opposites, choice

In the Lovers, we meet the "other" for the first time and must learn how to relate to others. The Lovers represent union, both with another person and within ourselves, and the coming together of opposites. This card is about forming bonds and connections, in romantic relationships and also more generally. Relationships with others, whether close and lasting or fleeting, offer us opportunities for growth, for getting to know ourselves better and also for learning to focus on something beyond ourselves. Whilst it's tempting always to interpret this card in that context, it's important to remember that we also have a relationship with ourselves, and this card also symbolises integrating the masculine and feminine (we all have both, although we do not always express them equally) within ourselves. The angel shown in many of the more modern versions of the Lovers represents a mediating force, helping us to balance our inner and outer dualities. When we feel complete and accepting of ourselves, we can meet others as a more honest version of ourselves, avoiding the projections which can influence our relationships. Our active or masculine side is often directed by our feminine or unconscious side, and this card symbolises this dynamic and the way it guides our actions.

The shadow or reversed aspects of the Lovers might be difficulty trusting or opening up to others, refusing to accept conflicting aspects of ourselves, and also expecting another person to complete or heal us rather than taking responsibility for our own emotional wellbeing. It may suggest being in a relationship for the "wrong" reasons, such as a fear of being alone, or love as a destructive rather than a unifying force.

In a reading, this card can be easy to interpret – it indicates a relationship, the strengthening of a bond with a loved one, perhaps a commitment or even marriage. However, it can also indicate the need to make a choice, often between staying in your comfort zone or moving towards a new level of maturity. Sometimes it represents the need to bring the masculine and feminine, the active and receptive, sides of ourselves into balance.

# 7 THE CHARIOT

Keywords: action, momentum, power, focus, determination, achievement, purpose

The Chariot is the card of victory, of being in control and achieving your goals. It can mean bringing the opposing energies sometimes indicated by the Lovers under control, by force or otherwise, and using this energy to move forward in pursuit of your ambitions. The two animals pulling the vehicle depicted in the card are often different colours or trying to go in different directions. As the driver of the Chariot, you need to keep them in balance, for both are necessary to move forward. Driving such a vehicle at speed requires total control over the animals, and so this card symbolises strong willpower. The charioteer is the victorious hero, who conquers all that he sets out to conquer. This card indicates worldly success achieved through sustained effort. Its a card of determination and enthusiasm, and often indicates the potential for leadership and accomplishment. There is always movement with the Chariot, a constant moving forwards in a dynamic balance. The sphinxes or horses once again represent the dualities within us, thinking and feeling, and acting and reacting. The Chariot can symbolise our "persona", the mask we create as we grow up which allows us to deal with the outside world and hide the parts of ourselves we are not so comfortable with.

The reverse or shadow side of the Chariot may be controlling yourself or others too much, or not enough, and having little sense of purpose or direction. It may also mean trying too hard to achieve a goal which is not right for you at this time. You may need to change your perspective or path, rather than following a course simply because it's the one you are already on.

When the Chariot comes up in a reading, you are likely to be in pursuit of a goal, probably with single-minded focus and a sense of purpose. Success is secure as long as you keep the momentum going, and keep your inner and outer selves, your thoughts and emotions, in balance. This is the card of the ego, which organises and controls our persona and allows us to act in the world but can become rigid and fearful if we are not careful.

# 8 STRENGTH

Keywords: inner strength, compassion, gentle control, patience

Like the Chariot, the Strength card symbolises willpower and our ability to control the circumstances around us and use them to our advantage. However the strength represented here is not forceful control or power over others, but rather power from within, a kind of gentle control which is patient and tolerant of the needs and desires of others. This card usually shows a woman who has tamed a lion or other wild beast, which allow her to touch it. The animal symbolises our inner "wild side", our animal instincts. Our strength and power come from those instincts and this card symbolises the power to use them wisely, rather than allowing them to take over, so that we act without conscious consideration. In some ways this card can be seen as balancing our conscious minds with our unconscious instincts, to make the best use of both of them. This is a strength of "allowing" rather than forcing, of using our inner rather than our physical powers. We can follow and fulfil our desires without allowing them to take us over or to hurt others, by transforming the devouring energies of our inner wildness into something in harmony with our higher self. The strength shown here is the strength to face life, especially when we are faced with challenges or change, with hope, able to see the opportunities or growth rather than becoming overwhelmed or giving up.

The reverse or shadow aspects of this card can be a lack of self-control, courage or integrity, being forceful or aggressive, and also losing focus and scattering your energy. It can also mean a lack of self-belief or loss of confidence in yourself.

In a reading, this card shows that you have this strength, and do not need to force others to bend to your will. Instead, you can inspire others with your tolerance and compassion. You can be guided by your instincts without being overtaken by them. This is a time to balance action and the urge to move forwards with intuition and the need for patience. You may be becoming aware of the power of your emotions and the need to use it consciously.

# 9 THE HERMIT

Keywords: solitude, inner wisdom, truth, patience, experience

The Hermit card shows a mature figure, carrying a lamp which symbolises inner wisdom, the knowledge we have built up with our life experience, which we can now use to light our way. The Hermit is a contemplative figure, who looks inwards and reflects on his knowledge in order to find the way forward. He is not in a rush and knows that true wisdom takes time. In fact the Hermit also symbolises the past, and old age, the power of time to bring change and growth. After the worldly cards of the first stages of the Fool's journey, now the Hermit asks us to draw on our inner strength and look within, to explore our own unconscious minds, to figure out what is most meaningful to us and use that awareness to guide our choices. He holds his lamp in his right hand, symbolising this conscious awareness of our inner wisdom. The Hermit symbolises humility before a higher power, and he knows that the more he learns, the more he realises he doesn't know. The Hermit is another powerful and deep-rooted archetype, and throughout history, people have withdrawn from society in order to contemplate the greater mysteries, like the medieval hermit living in a cave or the woods. On a symbolic level, the Hermit represents the idea that by withdrawing from the demands and concerns of the outer world, we can connect more deeply to our inner world. The Hermit asks us to consider where we are focusing our attention and energy, and whether it is truly worth our time.

The shadow or reversed aspects of the Hermit can be a feeling of isolation or loneliness, feeling uncomfortable with your inner self and unwilling to look within. You may find yourself taking refuge in meaningless activities or spending time with others to avoid the unsettling call of your higher wisdom.

When the Hermit appears in a reading, he indicates a time of quiet, calm introspection, even solitude. You are likely to be seeking something, perhaps a greater understanding of your life so far or your future path, or simply a deeper awareness of your place in the universe. It may be time to reevaluate your priorities, values and goals, especially if they are not allowing you to grow.

# 10 THE WHEEL OF FORTUNE

Keywords: cycles, change, ebb and flow, ups and downs

The Wheel of Fortune is a traditional image showing the ups and downs of life – sometimes the circumstances around us are positive and things seem to go our way, and at others times we may struggle or feel that we are unable to make progress. Often we do not have any control over these changes, and so the meaning of this card is also acceptance, as well as fate or destiny. This card can symbolise the natural rhythm of life, the season of growth and the season of fallow energy, and the awareness that both are necessary to keep us in balance. The Wheel teaches us when to go with the flow, when to endure, and how to understand out situation deeply enough that we know which of these approaches will serve us best. We are part of something bigger than ourselves, and an awareness of the Wheel of Fortune can give us a glimpse of this greater pattern. In history and mythology, the Wheel of Fortune can symbolise both the natural and mysterious laws of the universe, the seemingly random events of life, and also our attempts to influence those laws and change our apparent fate. As the halfway point of the Major Arcana sequence, the Wheel shows us how our lives are balanced between elements that we can control and a kind of fate or destiny which is more mysterious.

The reversed or shadow aspects of the Wheel of Fortune can be procrastination and passivity, assuming that our fate is out of our hands and there is nothing we can do to change it. Fighting or resisting necessary change can also be a negative manifestation of this card.

In a reading, the Wheel can indicate a time of change, a period when things seem to be happening beyond your control and you have no choice but to go with them. On the other hand, it can indicate a time when you feel stuck and don't seem to be able to move forward. Either way, the message of this card is often that whilst we may not be able to choose the circumstances around us, we can choose how we react to them and use the energy available to us.

# 11 JUSTICE

Keywords: balance, integrity, harmony, right action, equilibrium

As you might expect, Justice is the card of right and wrong, or right action and the repercussions of our actions. It can symbolise the structures around this in our society, such as the law, but on a deeper level, it speaks of our ethics and morality, the need to act with integrity and honesty. It symbolises impartiality, fairness, balance and objectivity, the need to act from our head, not from our heart. The principles of social or legal justice are more correctly ruled by the Emperor, whereas the Justice card represents a kind of cosmic equilibrium, the forces which keep the universe in balance as well as our individual lives. This can be a card of karma, of accepting that all of our choices and actions have consequences and that even if they are unintended, they are still our responsibility. This can be a liberating process, as it frees us from constantly repeating the same life patterns until we have learned the lessons of that past behaviour, and Justice brings us an awareness that our apparent free will is shaped by our past actions. Justice doesn't simply ask that we balance all the dualities and contradictions within us, but accept that each has something to teach us. We need to listen to and accept all viewpoints, to acknowledge them all as equally valid. The objectivity of Justice helps us to understand the ups and downs of the Wheel of Fortune and to bring those extremes into harmony.

The reversed or shadow aspects of Justice can be refusing to take responsibility for our actions or to accept the consequences of our decisions, and also leaping ahead to make a decision without considering all the facts. Acting from our heart rather than using our head is also relevant here.

In a reading, the appearance of the Justice card may indicate the need to make a decision, or perhaps to consider the causes and effects of your actions. It indicates a need to take responsibility and to act with integrity, doing what we know to be right rather than what is easy. When we see the Justice card, we need to consider how to honour our contradictions and bring ourselves into harmony.

## 12 THE HANGED MAN

Keywords: release, surrender, shift in perspective, sacrifice, suspension

The Hanged Man is a mysterious figure, unsettling to some as he appears to be in an uncomfortable position. However, in most of the images of this card, he looks peaceful and even happy. The Hanged Man is a paradox, for he teaches us that sometimes, the best way to succeed is to stop trying. After the turning inward of the last few cards and the uncomfortable truths we may be discovering about ourselves, the Hanged Man brings a period of peace. We need to suspend our actions for a while, reverse our perspective and surrender to what comes. This is a card of knowing when the time is right, and not doing anything until that time. The power of the Hanged Man lies in his stillness, his openness to a new way of being, and his ability simply to wait for the right time. He teaches us to re-frame our experience, to seek the positive in a challenging situation or the reality of an illusion. He can also show us our place in the bigger picture, allowing us to see beyond our individual concerns and connect to something greater than ourselves. This new perspective can allow us to sacrifice some of those individual concerns, especially those which are proving to be meaningless and make space for a clearer sense of who we really are. The Hanged Man can bring a kind of independence of thinking, an ability to release our social conditioning and follow the path of our hearts.

Reversed or shadow aspects of this card include holding on to a way of being which no longer serves us or refusing to consider change. We may not be willing to make the necessary sacrifices which will allow us to move forward, or we may sacrifice too much of ourselves or take on a victim mentality.

When he comes up in a reading, the Hanged Man tends to indicate a time when trying or taking conscious action to change our situation will not help. We need to release, to let go of our urge to control and allow events to unfold as they will. This is a card of patience and stillness, of allowing ourselves simply to be.

## 13 DEATH

Keywords: release, endings, transformation, change

Many fear this card, and perhaps with good reason, for it carries a powerful energy. It rarely indicates a literal death, but it does mean a change, a process of release and transformation which we must allow to happen if we are to move forward. Endings inevitably bring sadness, but almost every image of this card shows a new dawn beyond the skeleton, a new beginning on the horizon. In most cases, the changes heralded by the Death card are natural changes, for ultimately death is simply a part of life, one of life's few inevitablilities. The cycle of life, death and rebirth is the foundation of all things, and it must be acknowledged as such. The Hanged Man brings us to an awareness of what we need to release, and the Death card describes that process of release. It may be messy and painful, it may be a relief and a source of joy, but either way it is powerful and brings about deep transformation. We live in a world that often encourages us to ignore what is difficult, but it is there that the greatest power and potential lies. Death is usually seen as something to be feared, but it is actually the unknown that we fear, for who can really know what happens after we die? Symbolically, our ego resists change because of this same fear of the unknown. The image of dawn in the background of the card shows the positive potential of the unknown, the chance to experience life in all its glory.

The shadow or reversed aspects of the Death card can be resistance to change, stagnation and inertia, and holding on to worldly power or possessions to avoid the challenge of transformation and growth.

In a reading, the Death card indicates a process of inevitable change, and the need to acknowledge it rather than resisting or fighting against it. Whether it's an outdated emotional pattern or a job we no longer enjoy, saying goodbye to the past is the only way to move into our future. Sometimes we may be held back by unresolved feelings from our past, and acknowledging and releasing these clears the space for a new beginning.

## 14 Temperance

Keywords: balance, harmony, union of opposites, health

Temperance brings a calm energy after the powerful transformation of Death, a sense of inner union which comes from having faced our fears. Often shown as an angel pouring water between two containers, Temperance brings a sense of equilibrium and flow. She represents the principle of guiding and blending the dualities we have confronted in the last few cards, combining them to produce a sense of harmony. We are able to combine spontaneity with the knowledge we have gained so far and move beyond the restrictive masks of the ego self. The word "Temperance" comes from the Latin "temperare" which means "to mix" or "to combine properly". We do not just throw everything in together, we allow the process of combining to flow in its natural sequence. Like so many others in the second Septenary, this a card of allowing energies to flow rather than trying too hard or forcing them. Change comes when the time is right when all the pieces are in the right place and can come together in the most productive way. This card is often linked to rainbows, for example through the iris flowers shown in the image below and the resemblance of the angel to the Greek goddess Iris, goddess of the rainbow. The rainbow is a symbol of new life, of something magical seemingly created from nothing. It shows the energy of life which comes after the process of Death, our new awareness of our connection to the greater universe.

Reversed or shadow meanings of this card include being self-centred or going to extremes, mood swings or unstable actions, chaos or lack of self-control. Temperance reversed can indicate that you keep the various parts of your life too separate and risk becoming fragmented or losing a sense of who you are as a whole person.

When it appears in a reading, the Temperance card can mean a need for moderation or balance, for not going to extremes. It can indicate a time when we are in our "flow", able to connect to a deeper sense of self and act from that, bringing creative energy and a sense of being in touch with our true self. This card can also relate to health and a sense of wellbeing.

# 15 THE DEVIL

Keywords: power, bondage, freedom, materialism

The Devil is another card which many find challenging, with its often unsettling images of a horned figure presiding over two figures in chains. However look closer and you'll see that the chains are loose, and that the figures could remove them if they chose. Whilst this card can indicate feeling trapped or controlled, it also shows us that we have the ability to break our bonds. Often the Devil symbolises our shadow side, the parts of ourselves that we prefer to deny or ignore. We may be overly concerned with appearances or social status, with things that are not really meaningful and which take our power away from our spiritual growth. The Devil symbolises not only a focus on the material and meaningless, but also the illusion that nothing exists beyond that, a denial of the gifts and mysteries of spirit. The illusions of the material realm limit and restrict us, and can become addictions, in extreme cases. They do not bring true satisfaction, and so we keep going, thinking that the next shiny new thing will be the one that finally makes us happy. Once we acknowledge these feelings and the futility of this quest, we are released and can use the energy we reclaim for something genuinely meaningful. Like the Death card, facing our fears and challenges here is a powerful experience, one that can transform us deeply. The Devil card signifies the life force which we lock away in our shadow side or unconscious mind, and the ability to unlock it.

The shadow or reversed meaning of the Devil tends to mean giving in to our shadow side, focusing only on the shallow or superficial and ignoring the pull of anything deeper. On the other hand, it can mean the process of releasing our chains and taking back our power, acknowledging the shadow self.

In a reading, the Devil asks us to look to our power, and where we give it away. It may indicate that we are too caught up in the material and are neglecting our deeper self, or that we are ignoring our true self in an attempt to conform to the expectations of others. Either way, we are called to break our bonds and release our power.

## 16 THE TOWER

Keywords: breaking down, release, revelation, structures

Another unsettling card, the Tower shows figures being struck by lightning and falling from a high tower. It can indicate unexpected and even unwelcome change and upheaval or crisis over which we have no control. It often reflects the truism that bad luck seems to come in phases so that everything happens at once and we are left floundering as we try to deal with it all. On a deeper level though, it symbolises the need to break out of the structures we have built for ourselves, to change outdated patterns which no longer serve us. Having faced our shadow in the Devil, the structure of our ego may have taken a blow, as we are forced the confront the walls we have built around ourselves. As these walls shatter, we may feel that we are left stranded, our sense of security and safety gone. However, when we open our eyes and look around, we realise that we can see further than we have ever seen before and that new possibilities, things we might not have even imagined, are opening up before us. The Tower symbolises an awakening, a time when illusions are shattered and seemingly permanent structures are proved to be flimsy or false. Whilst this can be distressing, now you have the opportunity to build something stronger, and also more flexible, in accordance with your own values instead of the expectations or needs of others. This card can also symbolise a flash of insight or even enlightenment, a breaking open of awareness which gives us a much broader view of life.

The reversed or shadow meanings of the Tower include avoidance of change, refusal to understand or allow your awareness to grow, and holding on to rigid attitudes and entrenched ideas. It can also suggest a milder version of the upright meaning, a less dramatic version of necessary changes.

When the Tower comes up in a reading, it inevitably indicates a time of change. Whilst this can be unsettling or even painful, it also usually brings revelation. We are broken out of our comfort zone, and possibilities open up around us. It's time to let go of what no longer works and build something more fulfilling.

## 17 THE STAR

Keywords: hope, optimism, trust, faith

A time of calm follows a time of upheaval. The Star brings a sense of relief and a renewed sense of trust and faith in the universe. The pool often shown in this card represents our connection to something greater than ourselves, and we can tap into this when we are in need of reassurance or inspiration. The Star symbolises hope and optimism, a sense that we are on the right path. The light of the Star is the light of understanding, awareness, and truth, stimulating our imagination and our sense of connection to something greater than ourselves. The universe, spirit, the divine – however we think of it or define it, we are offered a continuous supply of wisdom, of energy for growth and understanding. The Star shines above us to guide our way, showing us a deeper sense of meaning and direction in our lives. The pool often shown in the Star card symbolises our connection to the unconscious mind, on both a personal and a collective level, and we can connect to the waters of the pool by tuning in to our still inner voice. The Star inspires us to bring the gifts of the unconscious into tangible reality, through our creative talents. Our inner transformation and newfound connection to the source of life (symbolised by the pool in the image) brings the potential to the way we work and act in the world. This is a card of inner calm and serenity, bringing healing and a holistic awareness. All the masks have fallen away (which is why the figure in this card is almost always nude), we know our place in the universe and our true self.

The shadow or reversed meanings of the Star include denying our talents and inner truths, losing ourselves in idealism without bringing our ideals into reality. It may mean insecurity, losing hope or taking a pessimistic attitude.

The appearance of the Star in a reading suggests an ability to connect to our deeper self and to trust that all will be well. Love and energy flow freely and are available to us as we need them, for ourselves or to share with others. This is a time to align ourselves with a higher consciousness, to grow in our connection to spirit, and to honour our creative imagination.

## 18 THE MOON

Keywords: cycles, imagination, shadow, illusion

The Moon can be a shadowy figure, indicating shadows and illusions as well as imagination and dreams. This card symbolises the unconscious mind and the darkness, which we often see as frightening. We fear the unknown, but it also brings great gifts of imagination and inspiration. The Moon symbolises the knowledge we hold deep in our cells, the embodied wisdom which goes beyond our intellect and connects us to our instincts and intuition. Intimately connected with our feeling self, the Moon asks us to listen to the wisdom of our emotions and to acknowledge their power. Delving deep into ourselves, we may encounter fears and delusions, perhaps old emotional patterns which no longer serve us and we can bring them into the Moon's gentle light and let them go. The Moon is connected with the cycles of growth and decay and asks us to pay attention to those cycles in our lives, learning when to let our energies build and when to release them. The darkness is just as important as the light, allowing us to nurture the seeds of new growth and also to rest and retreat when we need to. The Moon card always indicates the activity of the unconscious. This may be our personal unconscious minds, speaking to us through dreams, fears, and feelings, but may also be the collective unconscious. The Moon shows our connection to this more universal shadow, the aspects of it we connect to most deeply and how that connection affects us.

The shadow or reversed side of the Moon can be failing to acknowledge our feelings, imagination and sensitivity, ignoring the shadow, or paying too much attention to illusions and allowing them to rule us. Ignoring the pull of the unconscious means that it will simply try harder to get your attention, which can lead to distorted emotions and fears.

In a reading, the Moon suggests that this is a time when linear thinking will not work. Instead, you need to go with the flow, to follow your intuition and to let your inner voice guide you. It may be a time of psychic or intuitive awakening when you are learning to listen to new forms of knowledge. You may need to be careful not to be overwhelmed with fears or anxieties. Your instincts can guide you to know what is real and what is an illusion.

## 19 THE SUN

Keywords: creativity, enlightenment, confidence, optimism, joy

The light of the Sun can literally bring enlightenment, a sense of clarity and vitality which revitalises and energises us. This is a card of confidence and creativity, of letting yourself shine and of having your achievements recognised. It can be a card of understanding, enthusiasm and positive energy, and of getting to the heart of the matter. The Sun gives us vital and constant energy, a micro-regeneration each day which allows us to work in, and on, the warmth and light of our conscious growth. This is another card of good health (along with Temperance), of feeling invigorated, charged up and full of enthusiasm. There's a reason that so many cultures honour the Sun as a god or goddess, for it brings life to the earth, and on a symbolic level, consciousness to the self. Rather than a card of the controlling ego, the Sun symbolises our true, authentic self, without the masks or personas we sometimes rely on, hence the nudity of the child often shown in the card. The child is our inner child, the pureness of our being and the horse often ridden by the child symbolises power and vital force, the ability to move forward with confidence along our life's journey. In the Sun we are aware of the beauty of life, understanding the power of the life force in all its manifestations, experiencing life as pure energy. We feel joy, optimism and a sense of wonder, and radiate these feelings to those around us.

The reversed or shadow aspects of the Sun can be ignoring our inner child, a fear of trust or lack of confidence in ourselves. The Sun reversed suggest surviving rather than thriving, and a need for more illumination in our lives. The positive energy of the Sun is not lost but may become confused and less clear.

The Sun showing up in a reading is generally seen as a very positive omen, indicating a time when you are clear in your purpose, understanding and ability to shine. Masks have been set aside and you are able to let your true self shine through. You may find yourself the centre of attention, encouraging and inspiring others. It may also indicate a time of strong vital and physical energy.

## 20 JUDGEMENT

Keywords: inner calling, rebirth, awakening, forgiveness

Judgement is a card of awakening, of becoming aware of a higher purpose or calling which inspires you. There is an inner conviction, a sense of something you have to do, even – especially – if it is difficult or challenging in your current circumstances. The angel blowing the trumpet which features in many depictions of this card is the summons which calls us to a higher consciousness, a new level of awareness. This call is within us, a kind of yearning which bubbles up and demands attention, and also experience it as something outside us, coming from a force much greater and more mysterious than ourselves. The Judgement card symbolises rising up out of the restrictions of self-doubt and the expectations of others, bringing a kind of rebirth, the opening up of a new sense of self. Judgement can show you your true vocation or purpose in life, asking you to listen for what makes your soul sing and then find a way to follow that path. It can be challenging, but the potential rewards are great. This card can also indicate a more literal kind of judgement, perhaps a time of evaluating your life and making some necessary changes or releasing and guilt or sorrow we carry from the past so that we can move forward. Often we judge ourselves much more harshly than we judge others so this card is as much about forgiving ourselves as it is about forgiving others.

The reversed or shadow meanings of the Judgement card include being critical or judgemental of ourselves or others, and feeling disconnected from our spiritual awareness and stuck in the material, refusing to hear the call or trying to ignore it. It may also mean that you want to answer the call, but don't know what to do or where to begin.

In a reading, the Judgement card can indicate a time of rebirth, of answering the inner call, following the yearning of your heart to find fulfilment and a sense of purpose. Sometimes it indicates a literal judgement to be made, a truth to be found or a decision to be made. There is an energy of regeneration inherent in this card, which brings hope and the opening up of new possibilities.

## 21 THE WORLD

Keywords: completion, integration, accomplishment, fulfilment

The World is a card of completion, of everything coming together to achieve something that is greater than the sum of its parts. As the final card of the Major Arcana, it brings together the energies of all the previous cards, synthesising and integrating them. It symbolises wholeness, happiness and a deep sense of connection. This is not a static energy, but a dynamic balance. We are connected to the dance of life, free of the fears and doubts which may have held us back in the past and able to see both ourselves and the world around us more clearly. The World is the last numbered card of the Major Arcana, and as the end of the cycle, implies the beginning of the new one. This is why the Fool is sometimes referred to as card number twenty-two, as once we have reached the unity of the World, we step once more into our clearest, most spontaneous self, and begin again the spiral of growth. Like the universe, we are in constant movement, always part of the cycles of our inner self as well as the great cycles of the universe around us. The figure in the World card is the cosmic dancer, often seen as androgynous, having finally united all the dualities within. S/he moves with the cycles, endlessly flowing, transforming and renewing. The World and the Fool are the only two cards in the Major Arcana which show moving figures, connected to the great spiral of being which is part of us all, and of which we all form a part.

The shadow or reversed meanings of the World can be a refusal to acknowledge that a cycle has come to an end, stagnation and a refusal to move on, or keeping yourself isolated and cut off from the rest of the world.

When it appears in a reading, the World indicates the end of a cycle, the fulfilment of a goal, a dream realised. This is a time of satisfaction and contentment, of gratitude for what you have and the results of your efforts. When the World card comes up, it reminds us that we are part of something much bigger than our daily concerns and individual lives, and connects us to planetary and even cosmic consciousness.

# CHAPTER THREE: THE MINOR

# ARCANA

## THE STRUCTURE OF THE MINOR ARCANA

The Minor Arcana consists of four suits, each containing fourteen cards, numbered Ace through to Ten and then Page, Knight, Queen and King. Each suit connects to one of the four elements, fire, air, water and earth. According to traditional occult symbolism, each element represents a different area of life. Through the elemental energies, the cards of the Minor Arcana show the energies which play out in our everyday lives.

The suit of Wands connects to the element of fire. It symbolises action, passion, vision and creativity. Cards in the suit of Wands often relate to our work or other projects we put energy into.

The suit of Swords connects to the element of air. It describes the realm of the mind, our thoughts and ideas, and the way we communicate them with others. Traditionally the suit of Swords has symbolised conflict, and so some of the images can be unsettling, but conflict is only one of the meanings of the Swords cards.

The suit of Cups is linked to the element of water, the element of feelings, emotions and the imagination. The Cups cards show us the realm of dreams and the unconscious as well as the way we feel about and relate to others.

Finally, the suit of Pentacles brings it all into the realm of the material, the element of earth. The Pentacles cards deal with money, home and work, but also with our resources, values and sense of abundance.

## THE JOURNEY THROUGH THE NUMBER CARDS

Each of the numbers carries its own symbolism, and in combination with the element of the suit decides the meaning of the card. In general, the even numbers are harmonious whilst the odd numbers bring challenges. The basic numerological meanings are as follows:

- The Aces are the spark, the new beginning. They introduce the basic energy and message of the suit and are often seen as a divine gift.

- The Twos are a decision or a balance to be found, a need to integrate the dualities in our lives.

- Threes are the creation of something new, the opportunity to manifest the energy sparked by the Ace.

- Fours are the building of a solid structure and represent the natural order.

- Fives bring change and chaos and may bring tests and challenges.

- The Sixes bring balance and equilibrium, a sense of wholeness or completion.

- The Sevens bring a yearning for deeper connection, a process of initiation or transformation.

- The Eights connect us to rhythm and harmony, but also demand that we choose our priorities.

- Nines are the peak of their suit and can represent success and completion.

- The Tens are the end of the cycle, containing within them the seeds of the next cycle.

# THE COURT CARD FAMILIES

The Court card families, based on a rather medieval hierarchy of Page, Knight, Queen and King, are the "personality" cards of the tarot. The Page embodies the childlike, innocent experience of the elemental energy, and is often a messenger or student. They are learning about their element and are often absorbed in it. The Knight is on a quest to understand the energy of the element and to take it out into the world. They are seekers and explorers, always hoping for an adventure. The Queens hold the energy of their element, transforming it from within and inspiring others to do the same. The Kings are the masters of their element, wielding it in the world with authority and using their experience to help others. In a reading, Court cards can represent an actual person who is part of the querent's life, somebody influential who may affect the querent's experience or choices. They can also symbolise an aspect of the querent themselves, or a role they are playing or an energy they are embodying at the time of the reading.

# THE SUIT OF WANDS

## *ACE OF WANDS*

The Ace of Wands is the creative spark, an exciting new possibility opening up for you. The lightning rod of the Ace of Wands channels and focuses the energy of fire, making it available for the querent to follow their passion, create something new, or find a new and inspiring vision to carry them forwards. The divine gift of the Ace is a sense of optimism and purpose, and also a sense of meaning, of why we do what we do. We open up to new experiences and find meaning as well as pleasure in them, and perhaps a new sense of direction. This card can indicate listening to your intuition and becoming aware of a more spiritual side of life and to your self. It may mean the beginning of a process of spiritual development or a new level of creative experience.

## TWO OF WANDS

This can be a card of making a decision, of moving forwards towards a new goal. However it begins with preparation and evaluation, and so this card may indicate a need to consider your options, to look at all of your possible futures and choose your direction. The Two of Wands indicates that you are moving into your personal power, able to move forward with courage and originality and that the potential of the Ace is beginning to take form. This may mean moving out of your comfort zone, and the decision demanded by this card may be simply that, to move away from the familiar and onto a new path. When the Two of Wands comes up, it suggests that you are feeling restless, and there is a need to honour that restlessness, to prepare for movement even if you are not actually ready to move yet.

## THREE OF WANDS

The Three of Wands is a card of expanding your vision and exploring the unknown. It can indicate that you have achieved quite a lot already and that now is the time to evaluate those achievements and decide which of them to build on. You have stepped onto the path and maybe even travelled some way down it and now is the time to decide where it will lead you next. The Three is always a number of integration and the Three of Wands asks for the integration of what has gone before with what will come next. This means looking at the bigger picture and perhaps considering what is still unknown to you, calling on all of your knowledge and experience to see as clearly as you can. The Three of Wands is a card of foresight and also leadership, for in making your own choices you can inspire others to do the same.

## FOUR OF WANDS

The structure of the Four is seen as positive in the suit of Wands, as it contains the fire safely whilst also allowing it to burn consistently, for as long as it is fed. This card represents celebrations, home and a sense of security which brings contentment and excitement. These things fuel your inner fire, helping you to feel safe and confident enough to explore our creative self and to reach for your goals. This card can also indicate a time of rest, of gathering in the harvest of work done so far and enjoying the results before moving into the next phase. Four of Wands energy is productive and constructive, the energy of plans put into action and carried out successfully. Good results bring confidence and a sense of inner strength, a solid foundation which helps us to move forward.


## FIVE OF WANDS

The combination of the chaotic Five and the difficult to control energies of fire bring competition, minor annoyances which can cause stress or disruption, and a lack of focus. Your confidence and self-belief may be challenged and competition with others may cause confusion. There may be conflicting values or competing demands, leading to stalled progress and frustration. However, the chaos can also be helpful, allowing you to brainstorm creative strategies and solutions, finding a way to bring them together harmoniously and usefully. There may be tension or disorder, but these can be stimulants for growth and for a new way of thinking, as long as all parties involved are willing to be open and honest. The important thing is to accept that change is needed and work towards making the necessary changes. Denying the issue at hand will only compound it and lead to bigger problems.


## SIX OF WANDS

The Six restores harmony, and in the Six of Wands your achievements are finally recognised and the struggles of the previous card are resolved. It's a time when you can feel proud and enjoy the acclaim of others and the traditional meanings for this card include victory, conquest and success. It is a card of leadership, accomplishment and ambitions fulfilled, and also of the need to acknowledge the support of others in achieving your goals. Your victory is the result of your efforts and the efforts of those around you, a success that is earned and is all the sweeter for that. It symbolises the confidence that comes from using your abilities and talents not only for your own good but for the good of others, and the sense of satisfaction which follows. This brings a sense of ease and an ability to move forward into the future with confidence.


## SEVEN OF WANDS

The Seven of Wands symbolises courage in the face of opposition, the need to stand your ground and have the courage of your convictions. Following the success of the Six, new challenges appear. In most versions of this card, the figure holds the higher ground, symbolising the solid and positive position brought by past efforts and successes. However, the figure is usually also beset from all sides and may be outnumbered. When this card comes up, you may need to look at where you are on the defensive and where you have the strength to stand and fight. There may be a change you are resisting and sometimes letting go of the resistance is all that's needed to remove the obstacles to your progress. You may be called on to act with the courage of your convictions, and also to evaluate your priorities.

## EIGHT OF WANDS

The Eight of Wands signifies movement or rapid change, events which bring growth but which may feel rushed or as if your feet don't have time to touch the ground. In most versions of this image, the eight Wands are flying high in the air, carrying you into an exciting new future. The key is to use this energy to achieve your goals, without speeding ahead and losing sight of your priorities or focus. To others, it may seem as if you are moving for the sake of it, perhaps without necessary planning or thought, but to you, it most likely feels like you are "on a roll", and need to make the most of the momentum that is being generated for you. As well as action and movement, this card may mean receiving news which changes your situation, and lots of changes happening at once.

## NINE OF WANDS

This is a card of sustained effort and willpower, of not just finding your own path but creating each step as you go along. The work may feel challenging but also has the potential to bring great reward, as you are able to break old habits of excessive fear or caution. The energy of the Nines is quite self-contained, and this card can also mean the courage and energy to create your own destiny, rather than following convention or the expectations of others. This is not always an easy road, and there may be times when you are on the defensive, feeling frustrated at having to fight your corner over and over again. The key is taking responsibility for resolving any past issues which still affect you, and making space for healing rather than retreating into your comfort zone.

## TEN OF WANDS

The Ten of Wands is a card of commitment and dedication, having the determination to achieve your goals. It can mean giving service to something greater than yourself, such as family or the wider community, and accepting that the hard work and responsibility are worth it. It may mean that you have chosen your direction, and are happy to do whatever it takes to get there. However, it can also symbolise feeling burdened, as if you've taken on too much and can no longer see the way forward clearly. It may be time to let some commitments go, or at least to re-evaluate your priorities. The most important tasks are those which allow you to be true to yourself and to your higher purpose. Anything which doesn't serve those may need to be released or delegated, especially if you are only taking responsibility for it out of habit.

## PAGE OF WANDS

When the Page of Wands appears he brings opportunities to feed your passion and creativity. He encourages you to try something new, just for the fun of it. He is playful, curious, and always makes the choice which seems like the most fun. The Page is restless and may be easily distracted, because he is exploring, learning, seeking his path, and doesn't want to miss out on anything. All of these traits are part of a process of learning who he is and what his purpose is in life, and he is still at the beginning of this journey. The Page of Wands may need to acknowledge that he may not yet have the knowledge or experience he needs to define his goal more clearly. The key is to enjoy the process of gaining this knowledge and make the most of all the opportunities that come his way.

## KNIGHT OF WANDS

The Knight of Wands is an adventurer, setting off on a quest purely for the joy of taking action. He may enjoy taking risks and tends not to think before he acts. This is not because of a lack of intelligence, more that he is so inspired and enthusiastic about the task at hand that he cannot wait to get started, and so optimistic that he cannot see what might go wrong. He may come across as insensitive or intolerant because he is so focused on his quest that he is not aware of the needs or desires of others. He may also come across as somewhat erratic, as his energies burn fiercely whilst he is inspired by a task, but quickly dissipate when he loses interest until the next exciting quest comes along. He is likely to be very good at starting things, getting all fired up and passionate, but then losing interest when the initial excitement dissipates.

## QUEEN OF WANDS

A confident and passionate woman, the Queen of Wands is someone who encourages and inspires others with her creativity and enthusiasm. She has learned to hold the fiery energies within and release them when the time is right so that enthusiasm is sustained and the goal can be reached. She is independent and sure of herself, full of confidence but not arrogance, with enough self-awareness to encourage others without feeling threatened by them. Like all of the fiery Courts, at times she may seem domineering or even forceful, and she is likely to have little patience with those who are unwilling to take a risk. She takes a positive and optimistic approach and may get frustrated with those who she sees as unnecessarily negative or too fearful, perhaps not realising that not everyone can be as strong-willed as she is.

## KING OF WANDS

The King of Wands is an assertive and charismatic leader, willing to take chances and inspire action in others. He clearly expresses his creative imagination and is good at bringing his vision into reality. Unlike the Queen, he is not keen on working behind the scenes or in pursuit of someone else's vision, preferring to inspire others to help him bring his own vision into reality. He is good at influencing others and may become domineering, refusing to compromise his vision. He has little patience with those who do not share his confidence and determination, and his clear sense of focus. He will always take charge and shape the situation in the way that he wants or which advances his own plans. Sometimes he may struggle to understand that there are quieter forms of strength which are just as powerful as he is.

## THE SUIT OF SWORDS

## ACE OF SWORDS

The Ace of Swords brings a burst of mental energy, new ideas and a sense of clarity. The divine gifts of this Ace include reason, logic, intellectual thinking and mental discipline. The single sword cuts through mental and psychic clutter and brings a clearer vision, an ability to perceive the truth and to understand it. It brings a well of mental energy which can be focused on developing ideas and communicating them, and the growth of conscious awareness. This is a card of rational analysis and objectivity, the need to step back from emotions and view a situation dispassionately. It can also symbolise a sense of space, mental or otherwise, which allows new ideas to reach up into our conscious minds, bringing also the ability to understand them and decide what to do with them. The Ace of Swords connects us with the source of our ideas and also of our ability to communicate them with others.

## TWO OF SWORDS

When the Two of Swords appears, it may mean that you are feeling stuck or in a stalemate, not knowing how to move forwards or perhaps unable to make a decision. This card symbolises our inability or reluctance to see the truth or to deal with it, and possibly a refusal to change our opinion, blindfolding ourselves as the image often shows. Being closed off from others in this way can leave us isolated and lonely, or can give us the mental space we need to resolve the issues we are facing. Sometimes the message of this card is simply to make a decision. There is no right and wrong here, simply different choices, and we need to choose one of them and move on. Uncrossing the swords means reawakening the heart, and this card can be about the need to balance your thoughts with your feelings, the pull of logic with your emotions.

## THREE OF SWORDS

The Three of Swords is one of those cards that many see as difficult, as most of the images of it show a heart pierced by three swords. It's true that this card can mean painful feelings or a struggle with difficult emotions, but it can also mean releasing old emotional patterns and using our mind and intellect to understand our feelings. Sometimes we allow ourselves to be dominated by feelings which have actually moved on, or by fears which are no longer relevant. Applying the creative thinking of the Three of Swords allows us to see more clearly, and to realise that our feelings are simply that, our feelings, a part of us but not the whole of us. When this card appears, its time to acknowledge our feelings, and then let them go. This card can also symbolise bringing thoughts and feelings into creative harmony.

## FOUR OF SWORDS

The regularity and structure of the Four mean bringing your thoughts into harmony, clearing your mind of clutter and finding some mental space. You may need some time to process your emotions after the shifts of the Three, to practise not taking things personally and finding some objectivity. Taking time out allows us to get a sense of perspective, perhaps to reassess our priorities and make sense of our situation. This is a card of rest, retreat, taking time for reflection and contemplation, of letting go of our striving for a while. Every now and then we all need a little introspection, a time to step back from the demands of daily life and check in with ourselves. We do not always need to be "doing" and being productive, sometimes it's important just to be, with no goal or effort in mind.

## FIVE OF SWORDS

The image of the Five of Swords usually shows a man walking away from a battlefield, perhaps carrying several swords and with the others lying on the ground. The airy clarity of the Swords is lacking and the energy is turbulent and confused. This card can symbolise defeat, a battle lost, or won through deception. It asks you to check your motivation and state of mind. Are you focusing on your own needs at the expense of others, or seeking a balance between the two? When the Five of Swords appears, it can indicate a time of communication breakdown or a lack of clarity. There can be a need to choose your battles, to reassess your priorities and put your energy only into that which is most important. Otherwise, you may find yourself with scattered energy and scattered thoughts, lacking the focus to move forward and carry out your plans.

## SIX OF SWORDS

Once again the harmonious Six restores harmony after the chaos of the Five, and the image for the Six of Swords usually shows one or more people in a boat being ferried across calm waters. This card symbolises transition or evolution, the truism that change may not be dramatic and exciting but may come gradually, as we work on our inner and outer growth. The six Swords are carried in the ferry boat, and they may symbolise the inner truths or burdens you carry forwards with you or the established ideas which help you to make sense of life. They may also be interpreted as treasured possessions, past pain being held on to, or valuable resources with which to pay the ferryman. Either way, they are in some way necessary to the voyage and the transition into the next stage of life.

## SEVEN OF SWORDS

The traditional meanings for this card include secrecy and cunning, possible deception or not being able to see the whole picture. It can indicate taking a subtle or even hidden approach rather than acting openly, perhaps keeping your plans to yourself. Sometimes there is an element of mistrust and when this card comes up, it's important to check in with your own motivations and those of the people around you. It may simply mean that the time is not yet right to share your ideas. Whatever level this card is working on, it implies a time of solitude and relying on your own inner resources, acting independently rather than relying on the support of others. The Sevens always symbolise a process, an energy which grows over time, rather than a single event, and the Seven of Swords suggests a process of getting clear about your ideas and how you are putting them into action.

## EIGHT OF SWORDS

In contrast to the movement of the Seven, the Eight of Swords usually shows a figure who is standing still, often trapped and surrounded by swords. This card suggests that you are feeling powerless, restricted, or simply confused. There may be a sense of insecurity or self-doubt, perhaps a reluctance to make a choice due to lack of confidence or overthinking all the options. All of these things can restrict your thinking, leading to indecisiveness and an inability to break out of these habitual patterns of thought. However, we may be less trapped than we think. In most of the images of this card, the figure is only loosely tied around the arms and there are gaps between the swords. Sometimes all you need to do is make the choice to break out, and you will find its easier than you expect so that the Eight of Swords is also a card of liberation.

## NINE OF SWORDS

The Nine of Swords shows us the challenges of this process of liberating your mind from the thoughts that hold you back. It indicates a time when you may be allowing your worries or anxieties to take over, imagining the worst and struggling to clear your mind. Like the previous card, it shows the power of the mind and the effect it can have on you, holding back growth due to imagined doubts and often unfounded fears. When the Nine of Swords comes up, there is a need to clear the mind, perhaps doing something physical which allows you to bypass the busy thinking brain. Rather than giving equal energy to worries or concerns which may not even happen, its time to sort through them and work out which are genuine and which are simply old habitual patterns of feeling and thinking.

## TEN OF SWORDS

The Ten of Swords shows the end of the cycle, often illustrated by a figure lying on the ground, with all ten swords in their back. One of the meanings for this card can be having a victim mentality, believing that everything is against you in a rather dramatic way. However, the regeneration of the Tens is also shown, with the lightening sky of a new dawn often shown beyond the figure. There is a need to accept and release the past, to let go of the patterns of thinking which keep you pinned down, clearing the way for a new beginning. The Ten of Swords can show a time of gathering and replenishing your energies, of recommitting to your path. It can also mean taking your ideas out into the world, teaching or sharing them with others, which is of course also a kind of release.

## PAGE OF SWORDS

The Page of Swords is setting out on his journey to gain knowledge of himself and the world around him, to understand the world and his place in it. He is determined, self-willed and perhaps somewhat detached, not quite ready to form close relationships with others yet. Instead, he is keen to make his own way, to be allowed to make his own mistakes if necessary. He is exploring his ideas, concepts and seeking his own truth, using his intellect and the powers of his mind in quite an abstract way, as he doesn't yet have the life experience to do otherwise. When the Page of Swords appears, you are likely to be practising using your mental energy and ability to communicate with others. This card can symbolise messages and new ideas which bring a new level of awareness, perhaps studying or learning something new which expands your horizons.

# KNIGHT OF SWORDS

This Knight is on a quest to fight for the truth and welcomes conflict as an opportunity to get closer to that truth. He is courageous and clever, always ready to defend his ideas and his honour, and always on the move. He has strong powers of logic and reason, often seeing the world as black and white and acting accordingly. Quick thinking and even impulsive, he has the courage of his convictions, to the point that he may struggle to let go of an idea even when it is proved wrong. He thinks quickly but not necessarily deeply, and may choose action based on a half-developed idea over a carefully planned strategy. His insistence on logic and objectivity may mean that he lacks tact and empathy with others, sometimes riding roughshod over individuals and their needs in order to achieve his goal.

# QUEEN OF SWORDS

Honest and astute, the Queen of Swords tells it like it is and doesn't flinch from the truth. Ideally, she transforms sorrow into wisdom by applying her powerful intellect to her emotional experiences, finding a sense of perspective and an ability to see the bigger picture. Her experience meeting the ups and downs of life has brought resilience and courage, as well as empathy for others and a heart connection which is not always present in the Swords cards. She is able to use logic and reason to quash any self-doubts or confused thinking and to help others to do the same. She is quick-witted and has a love of ideas, along with the maturity to develop them fully and share her understanding and wisdom with others. The Queen of Swords makes decisions quickly and with compassion, and lives by her ideals.

# KING OF SWORDS

Articulate and intellectual, the King of Swords sees straight to the truth of the matter and has excellent analytical skills. He is an intellectual leader and keen strategist, always acting from high ideals, high standards and a deep level of experience and understanding. At times this may mean that he seems to lack compassion or tolerance, and he may consider the greater good to be more important than the needs of the individual. He is a trusted adviser, forthright and reliable, who is able to be realistic as well as idealistic. He stands for law, order, discipline and sound judgement, and as such may come across as a strong authority figure who does not like to be opposed. When the King of

Swords appears, its time to use your judgement and find some clarity about your situation, and then take decisive action.

# THE SUIT OF CUPS

## *ACE OF CUPS*

The Ace of Cups brings a rush of emotional energy or an opening up of the imagination. It can symbolise a return to the source of yourself, getting in touch with your unconscious mind through your dreams and intuition. There may be a new attraction or bond with another, an overflowing of feeling which feels exciting and full of promise. A new chapter is beginning in which relationships and connections with others, as well as connection to your own feelings and imagination, bring personal growth and a deeper connection to the spiritual side of life. This is a time to be open to new opportunities, to focus on and express your gratitude for what you have. You may be feeling a little vulnerable and sensitive, especially if there are strong emotional energies around you, so it's important to practise self-care and love yourself as well.

## *TWO OF CUPS*

When the Two of Cups appears, you may be making a soul connection with another, a union which allows you to grow on an inner level as well as an outer. This card can symbolise the beginning or deepening of a relationship, and also building and enjoying partnerships in a more general sense. You are likely to be feeling compassionate and empathetic towards others, able to appreciate their uniqueness and the gifts they bring to your life. The Two of Cups symbolises positive and helpful unions, the connections you make with others, especially one to one, which helps you to get to know yourself better. Meeting the other person as they really are, rather than as we want them to be, is really important with this card, otherwise you risk building relationships based on your own projections rather than a genuine connection.

## *THREE OF CUPS*

The Three of Cups traditionally symbolises friendships and social connections, feeling positive and enjoying life. Its a card of abundant emotions, celebrating with loved ones, and feeling content and happy. The gifts of joy and laughter bring just a much inner growth and change for us as do suffering and painful emotions, so this card asks you to make space in your life to feel and enjoy those positive emotions, and to take a light-hearted approach. On a deeper level, this card symbolises the emotional security which comes from knowing where you belong and feeling comfortable and able to be yourself. It's about finding your soul friends, the people who are family whether you are related to them by blood or not. The Three of Cups is a card of building and celebrating those connections and enjoying the deep emotional bond they bring.

## FOUR OF CUPS

When the Four of Cups appears, it indicates that you might be feeling stuck in a rut, perhaps somewhat self-absorbed or apathetic, unable to see the gifts life offers you. You may have a sense of dissatisfaction, perhaps feeling that something isn't quite right but not really knowing what to do about it. You may feel trapped in old emotional patterns, unable or unwilling to move out of them. The Four of Cups can indicate a necessary period of introspection, a time to get in touch with your feelings and process any past emotions which you no longer need and which may be holding you back. Past hurts can blind you to new opportunities, meaning that you hold yourself back in fear and remain in your comfort zone. Whilst it's understandable that you fear being hurt again, you also risk missing out on positive new connections.

## FIVE OF CUPS

The shifts and changes of the Fives, in the feeling realm of the Cups, can mean feeling loss or regret and needing to acknowledge painful emotions in order to begin the healing process. The Fives of Cups can indicate a time of grief or disappointment, of feeling let down or hurt by someone that we cared about, and needing to take the time to process the experience. It's important not to repress or ignore difficult feelings, or they have a tendency to reappear in a much more destructive form. On the other hand, this card also counsels against spending too much time wallowing in self-pity or blaming others for what has happened to you. Only you can make the choice to move on, and this card affirms that the time will come and that negative feelings do not define you.

## SIX OF CUPS

The traditional meanings for the Six of Cups include nostalgia, childhood, and innocence. You may find yourself thinking about the past, about the influence it had on your growth and the choices you made in life. This can be helpful, if you use your memories creatively, but can also lead to viewing life through rose-tinted spectacles. Sometimes the past is idealised and it's important to appreciate all the experiences, good and bad, which made you the person you are today. Attending to unfinished business is useful, as long as it doesn't hold back your current growth. On a deeper level, this card can symbolise getting in touch with our inner child, perhaps rediscovering y creativity or ability to play and finding new ways to express your true self. The Six of Cups invokes positive feelings of kindness and generosity, empathy and compassion for others.

## SEVEN OF CUPS

The seven of Cups is traditionally seen as a card of daydreaming and wishful thinking, of having so many options that you are unable to settle on any of them. The seven Cups in the image are often shown full of various items which may tempt us, such as jewels, fruits, the snake which symbolises regeneration or the laurel wreath which symbolises victory. When the Seven of Cups appears, you may be feeling that you want it all, or that you have no idea what you want. The Seven of Cups can symbolise illusions and an excess of imagination. This is a card of abundance, but it also indicates a need for discernment, for looking closely at each option and deciding whether it is superficial or meaningful, something that we truly want or something that is imposed on us by others. This discernment is necessary to bring the products of your imagination into tangible reality.

## EIGHT OF CUPS

As with all of the Eights, the Eight of Cups brings an urge to reestablish harmony, a need to get back in touch whatever is most meaningful in your life. This may mean taking some time for introspection, to decide what that is and how to change your life to accommodate it. This card is often the beginning of a journey of inner discovery, moving on from what you have built so far to seek higher wisdom and deeper understanding. This may mean giving up parts of your life to which you have become attached, to give up on goals or plans which are no longer fulfilling or inspiring. This may not be popular with those around you and may mean going against the expectations of friends, family or mainstream society. The Eight of Cups is therefore also a card of being true to yourself, even if it means making some painful decisions.

## NINE OF CUPS

The Nine of Cups is often known as the "wish card", as it symbolises emotional and physical satisfaction, of having your wishes and dreams fulfilled, and enjoying the results of your hard work. It's a card of enjoying the pleasures of the senses, which may mean connecting more meaningfully to your emotions, or may mean ignoring them, especially the challenging ones. There is a sense of complacency about this card, a smugness and self-satisfaction which suggests a disconnection from others. Most versions of this card show a solitary figure, suggesting someone who is unable or unwilling to share their success. Whilst is good to enjoy the results of your hard work and the happiness you have earned for yourself, enjoying it alone may not be satisfying for long. This card symbolises the rewards of generosity and shared abundance, the realisation that holding your happiness for yourself limits it, whereas sharing it with others increases it.

## TEN OF CUPS

The Ten of Cups brings a deep sense of emotional fulfilment and emotional security, an awareness of the abundance and blessings of life. Most of the images for this card show a happy family or couple, secure in their deep connection and love for each other. This card indicates a sense of belonging to family or tribe, an appreciation of the support of others and the willingness to support others yourself. The Ten of Cups is a card of inspiration, love and harmony, of dreams coming true through your own sustained efforts. It carries a sense of "coming home" in an emotional sense, of discovering where you belong and the people you belong with. Whereas the Nine of Cups suggests outer satisfaction, the Ten of Cups brings inner satisfaction, not just material abundance but emotional abundance too. You are able to see beyond yourself and appreciate all the gifts life has brought you.

## PAGE OF CUPS

The Page of Cups is beginning a journey of acknowledging and revelling in his feelings, of understanding them and also simply feeling them, even allowing them to overwhelm him at times. He has a strong sense of imagination and a deep ability to love, although he may be quite naïve and innocent. He can be sensitive, but is loyal and trustworthy, and not afraid to be vulnerable. When this Page appears, you may need to open up and take an emotional risk, to let others see and understand the real you. It may be time to recognise and begin the work of understanding hidden emotions and intense feelings. Whilst this is easy for positive feelings such as joy and love, it's also important not to ignore the challenging feelings. The journey for this Page is the quest to feel all of our emotions,

however difficult and to appreciate their gifts.

## KNIGHT OF CUPS

The Knight of Cups is a romantic daydreamer, sensitive and fond of poetry and flights of fancy. In some ways he is the Knight closest to the chivalry and divine inspiration of medieval knights, risking all for love or for an idealistic dream. He feels intensely and may come across a quite dramatic at times, unable to see beyond his overwhelming feelings and his need to express them. He is charismatic, the kind of person others are drawn to, but may also be given to illusion or even deception, of himself as well as others. Unlike the Wand and Sword Knights, his horse is usually shown standing still, as for him the action and movement take place on an inner level. His quest is one of the heart, the quest for true love or devotion and service to a higher being or ideal.


## QUEEN OF CUPS

Kind and tenderhearted towards others, this Queen is empathetic and strongly in touch with her psychic side and her powerful imagination. She is sensitive and feels intensely, but has the power to hold these feelings and also to share them with others to inspire or reassure them. As well as being good at connecting to her own feelings, she can encourage others to acknowledge and express their own feelings and is likely to be seen as a caring and compassionate figure. She is closely connected with her dreams and intuition and is often shown with at least one foot in the waters of the unconscious. She symbolises emotional integrity, nurturing others with her love and care. She is often artistic and creative, seeking ways of expressing her emotions tangibly and in ways others can understand. She may also have a deep connection to the spiritual side of life.


## KING OF CUPS

A wise guide and counsellor, the King of Cups has a deep understanding of the emotional self and a strong sense of empathy. He has worked hard to gain mastery of the emotional realm and may put his skills to use as a counsellor or adviser for others. As with all the Kings, he carries the authority of the suit and takes responsibility for the realm of feelings and imagination. He understands and accepts that emotions are complicated, and this can make him detached, by choice or otherwise. Unlike his Queen, he is generally depicted standing or sitting completely on land, by the side of the water rather than in it. He chooses to stay disconnected in order to be able to heal, teach and help others, without getting drawn in or personally involved. He is creative but may be more focused on creating frameworks for helping others than on expressing his personal creativity.

## THE SUIT OF PENTACLES

### *ACE OF PENTACLES*

The Ace of Pentacles brings a divine gift of abundance which increases your possibilities for material security. It represents a surge of personal power and energy which you can use to increase your material abundance and build a more solid foundation for your endeavours. It may indicate a new awareness of a growing skill or talent, or new opportunities to practise those skills and talents. When the Ace of Pentacles appears, it brings favourable conditions for manifesting ideas, for starting a business or a new professional or artistic project. Everything may seem to fall into place so that suddenly you have all the resources you need, or a burst of inspiration may remind of resources that are already available to you. This Ace brings the potential for building a greater sense of self-worth and a feeling of inner as well as outer security.

## TWO OF PENTACLES

The Two of Pentacles symbolises the ability to be flexible and to find ways to balance all the demands that life makes of you. Most of the images for this card show a figure holding a pentacle in each hand, juggling or balancing them. Whether it's your job and your personal life, your family and your work or simply two different, equally demanding, projects, you may be finding that you are struggling to balance these different areas of your life. In the first place, the Two of Pentacles often simply affirms that you are able to do this, that you are learning to be flexible and how best to use your energies. This card asks you to enjoy the process and to appreciate the gifts and challenges of all of the different demands on your time and energy. Each is there for a reason and has something to teach you.

## THREE OF PENTACLES

When the Three of Pentacles appears, you may find yourself working with others in a team or group, making your contribution and enjoying the support of others. This is a card of shared effort, of coming together to build something that is greater than the sum of its parts. It can also symbolise the need and ability to ground your creative visions in physical work, to take the steps you need to bring your dream into reality. The Three of Pentacles indicates our skills, our mastery of them and our ability to use them to achieve our own and shared goals. It asks us to use them well, planning our work and working to our highest ability. This is a card of integrity, dedication and commitment. The Three of Pentacles also symbolises taking satisfaction and pleasure in our work, our ability to create something from nothing.

## FOUR OF PENTACLES

The fixed structure of the Four, in combination with the earthy energy of the Pentacles, creates something lasting and solid, and the ability to structure and organise your life. However taken too far, this can mean getting stuck in a rut, and sticking to the familiar, staying in your comfort zone and avoiding growth. It can also symbolise possessiveness, the urge to hold on to what we have, to cling to material possessions as the only means of security. This can mean that you close yourself off from a more meaningful life or a sense of something outside of yourself, leading to a limited vision or a perceived lack of possibilities. The Four of Pentacles can symbolise shelter and protection, which everybody needs, but can also indicate hiding in that shelter as a way of avoiding life. This card asks you to open up, to share what you have and to re-connect with the world.

## FIVE OF PENTACLES

The Five of Pentacles traditionally indicates a time of feeling insecure or lacking in support, a time when you are more aware of what you lack than what you have. Most of the images for it are of isolation or being left out in the cold, lacking in shelter or resources. Like all of the Fives, the Five of Pentacles indicates a time of transition, changes which may initially be prompted by outer circumstances but which lead to inner growth. The Five of Pentacles can be said to illustrate the dangers of relying too much on the material for your security. This can leave you spiritually bereft and lacking a sense of meaning so that the motivation to move forward and do something productive is lost. When the Five of Pentacles appears, its time to learn the lessons of the dark night of the soul and accept the support that is offered.

## SIX OF PENTACLES

The Six of Pentacles symbolises the process of giving and receiving, the exchange of energy which sustains us and those around us. This is a card of inner and outer resources, and of giving and taking, of learning to share what we have. You may be the wealthy merchant who is able to be generous or the poorer relation who needs to accept help. Many people actually find the latter more difficult, preferring to stay in the cold isolation of the Five rather than accept the extra support that may be offered. Whichever position you are in, this card asks you to take a look at your attitudes and habits around giving and receiving. Do you give out of genuine concern for others, or to make yourself feel better? Perhaps you are concerned that any help you accept might come with conditions or expectations. The Six of Pentacles brings a chance to gain awareness of these dynamics.

## SEVEN OF PENTACLES

The Seven of Pentacles often indicates a process of shifting the balance of your life away from material concerns and towards something more meaningful, for example moving from a job which pays the bills to a vocation which is more fulfilling and allows you to be true to yourself. It can also indicate a time to pause and allow your harvest to develop, reassessing or evaluating your situation. This card suggests an enjoyment of the work for its own sake, rather than a focus on the end goal or what you have achieved so far. Looking at what you have achieved so far brings its own rewards though, and this card indicates that you are beginning to see the results of your hard work and to make a genuine difference in the world. The Seven of Pentacles indicates that patience and determination are the recipe for success.

## EIGHT OF PENTACLES

The Eight of Pentacles symbolises sustained effort, the repeated practising of a skill or honing of a talent. When this card appears, you are more likely to be working for the joy of it rather than in expectation of reward, working to gain mastery of your craft for your own personal satisfaction. On one level, this card is simply about focusing on the task before you and doing your best, taking your time to do a good job. On a deeper level, it can be about finding your passion, the work or vocation which brings you the greatest fulfilment and which will become your life's work. Like the Seven, this card carries energies of patience, determination and persistence. The rewards take time, but that is part of what makes them worth having. This is a card of giving service, to your higher self as well as the greater good.

## NINE OF PENTACLES

The Nine of Pentacles brings the rewards of your own efforts and the sense of security which comes from having achieved your goals. This is a card of discipline, self-control and self-reliance, and of reaping the rewards of long application of those qualities. The images for this card usually show a solitary figure standing in a garden, which symbolises fruition and fulfilment. The Nine of Pentacles indicates a time when you can enjoy a sense of material security and the knowledge that you have achieved that for yourself, through your own hard work. This card symbolises wealth and abundance, success and satisfaction, all coming from a sense of dedication to purpose and a strong and clear focus. It can mean taking the time to enjoy what you have, feeling secure in your values and the comfort you have built for yourself.

## TEN OF PENTACLES

The Ten of Pentacles brings a sense of affluence and abundance, on a material but also at a deeper level. Rather than a solitary figure, most versions of this card show an extended family, perhaps several generations, indicating that this card can mean a legacy, the urge to pass on not just material security but also the wisdom and learning of a life well lived. As with the other Tens, this card indicates sharing the lessons of the suit with the community and passing on the lessons learned, in readiness for closing this cycle of growth and beginning a new one. The Ten of Pentacles symbolises the security of family and inheritance, and also the sense of belonging to something greater than ourselves. This card can indicate where your roots are, or where you choose to put them down, and also a connection to your ancestors and an awareness of how they have influenced your life, directly or indirectly.

## PAGE OF PENTACLES

The Page of Pentacles epitomizes lifelong learning, the idea that all of life has something to teach us, and also that learning is not just about the intellect. He is beginning a journey of learning from experience, through study but also through observation, experimentation and simply doing the work. When the Page of Pentacles appears, its time to start putting your ideas into practice, beginning with small steps and building your momentum. This Page is patient and determined, but also always busy, believing that its important for both mind and body to be well occupied. He seeks ways to make a tangible difference in the world and sees his learning as something to apply in a practical situation, rather than an abstract understanding. His work is to change outward experiences to inner understanding, and so sometimes he may appear self-absorbed.

## KNIGHT OF PENTACLES

The Knight of Pentacles embodies diligence and hard work, a reliable figure who is trustworthy and loyal. He symbolises structure and organisation, and also dedication and commitment. He takes responsibility and accepts his obligations without complaint, and is more likely to focus on fulfilling his duty than on a personal quest or individual project. Sometimes this Knight is seen as dull, staid or even rigid, as he represents the need for steady hard work, drawing on the traditions of the past rather than seeking innovation. However, he always gets the job done, fulfilling all of his goals and commitments. He takes a methodical approach and is always productive, preferring to work towards a specific purpose rather than for the sake of it. Sometimes he is seen as a farmer, working with nature and the seasons to ensure that all grows in its due time.

## QUEEN OF PENTACLES

This Queen is an earth mother figure who nourishes and nurtures, providing practical help and advice as well as emotional support. She is resourceful and trustworthy and inspires others to make the best use of their talents by making the best use of her own. She embodies the abundance of nature and the gifts of the earth, and in some ways can be seen as a more down to earth version of the Empress. Like the other Queens, she holds and transforms the energy of her suit, and then radiates it outwards, encouraging others to live by their values and in harmony with their environment. She embodies the truth that by living and working with integrity, we can find satisfaction in our work and that work in the material realm can be an important path to spiritual growth and personal integration.

## KING OF PENTACLES

The King of Pentacles is an enterprising person who has a natural head for business and is able to make the most of an opportunity. He is shrewd, good at planning and taking a long-term view, willing to work hard to maximise his growth over time. As the master of the earthly realm, this King symbolises the rewards of sustained effort and our achievements in the material world. He has material abundance and likes to enjoy it, but he doesn't lose sight of what is really important, valuing people and connections over possessions. He is a good leader, although he may tend towards a more traditional rather than an innovative approach, valuing the past and the lessons it can teach us. He has high standards and good judgement and expects others to maintain those just as well as he does.

# CHAPTER FOUR : HOW TO DO A TAROT

# READING

## TAROT SPREADS AND HOW THEY WORK

A tarot spread is a map, or layout, in which you place cards in specific positions. A spread can contain anything from one or two cards to the whole deck, but most spreads contain between three and twelve cards. The spread you choose will depend on the question you want to ask, and how detailed you would like the answer to be. A spread might be one or two cards first thing in the morning to give an overview of the energies of the day or a reading for a full year with one or more cards for each month.

When doing a tarot reading, whether for yourself or someone else, taking your time to set up your space is important, as it helps to shift your mood and open up your intuition. You may like to light some candles or incense, and lay the cards out on a nice cloth which is only used for tarot readings. All of these actions create a "ritual" around the cards, reminding us that doing a tarot reading as a meaningful and important experience. The little rituals we use as we begin a reading help to align our inner and outer realities and open us up to messages from the universe and from our higher self.

Most tarot readings start with a question, even if it's only a vague desire to know what is happening around you at the moment. Asking the right question can be key to a good tarot reading, and it's worth taking some time before you start the reading to word your question carefully. The tarot doesn't tend to answer closed questions or those with seeking yes / no answers very well. What do I need to know about my relationship with X? works better than Does X love me? or Is X the one for me? Its always best to focus the question, and therefore the reading, on the querent themselves, rather than a third party. If they are nor present, or even aware that the reading is happening, their energies do not come through so clearly. There is also a question of ethics here, as asking about a third party invades their privacy. Many tarot readers also prefer to avoid emotive questions regarding pregnancy, health or the law, and if a querent asks you about such matters it is perfectly acceptable and even advisable, to refer them to the relevant professional.

Once you have decided on your question, and the spread you want to use, the next step is to shuffle the cards. Everyone has their own way of doing this, and you'll discover yours as you gain experience. Many people like to "cut" the deck by splitting it into three piles and then re-stacking them in a different order. When you are satisfied that you have shuffled the deck sufficiently (as with so much of tarot reading, this is a matter for your intuition, and over time you'll come to know when its "enough"), lay the cards down one at a time in the order and positions given in the layout diagram.

When doing a reading, we consider the story the cards tell. Each card is interpreted individually, but also in the context of both its position in the reading and also the cards around it. Once you have laid out the cards, look at them all together. Are there any similarities or cards which link together? For example, there may be lots of Cups cards, several Major Arcana cards or no Major Arcana cards, or more than one card with the same number. By looking at the overview of the spread, we can get a sense of the general energies of the reading. Lots of Cups cards might mean a time of emotional changes or when the querent is ruled by their feelings. Lots of Major Arcana cards implies that this is an important question, even if it doesn't seem so on the surface, whereas no Major Arcana cards would suggest that this is an everyday concern, with a relatively straightforward solution or result. Looking at the colours in the cards can also give us valuable information. Are they all bright, all dark, or is there a contrast? If there are people in the cards, which direction are they looking in? Do they face each other or have their backs to each other? All of these visual clues awaken our intuition and help us to decide the meaning of the cards in the specific context of this reading and this question.

# THE THREE CARD SPREAD, WITH EXAMPLES

The three card spread is one of the most popular and has many variations. Three cards is a good balance between not overloading yourself or your querent with information, whilst still gaining enough insight to show you a way forward. Some of the most popular include:

- Past, present, future,
- Issue, action, outcome,
- Body, mind, spirit,
- Situation, opportunity, challenge.

The cards are usually laid out in a straight line, as shown above, but they may also be laid out in a triangular shape. Examples of two three card readings are given below.

This is a past, present, future reading, for the simple question "What do I need to know right now?"

The Tower is in the past position, the Ace of Cups in the present, and the Fool in the future. Two Major Arcana cards in a three card reading is a high percentage, so immediately we can see that although the querent is asking a very general question, she seems to be going through some important changes, and may be struggling to get a grasp on them. The Tower in the past position confirms this, suggesting that there may have been some drama for the querent in the last few months and that it may not have been something that she chose or was able to control. However, the Ace of Cups in the present position shows that even if those changes felt difficult at the time, the way has been cleared for a new beginning. It may not be clear yet what that will look like, but there is a flow of emotional energy and a connection to the powers of the imagination which brings a sense of possibility and potential. Again, this is confirmed by the Fool as the future card. This shows the querent embracing those new possibilities and moving out of her comfort zone to a brand new chapter of life. The structures of the Tower have broken down, bringing the querent the freedom to follow her bliss, perhaps to do something she has dreamed of or imagined (the Ace of Cups) but has never had the courage to do before. We can see this process by looking at the colours of the cards. The dark greys of the Tower can feel oppressive, but the Ace of Cups and the Fool are much lighter and clearer, reflecting the calmer energies around the querent as she moves away from the experience of the Tower.

The querent for this reading asked, "What do I need to know about my relationship?" The first card, the Two of Cups, shows the current Situation, the second, the Lovers, shows the Opportunity available to the querent, and the final card, the Empress, shows a potential Challenge the querent may face. Again, there are two Major Arcana cards, so this is likely to be an influential relationship for the querent, which brings growth and possibly some life changes. The Two of Cups in the Situation position shows that this may be quite a new relationship and that both parties are feeling a strong sense of a soul connection, an attraction with the potential to develop into something more. They are likely to be getting on well and discovering that they have lots in common. The positive potential of this card is reflected in the Lovers as the Opportunity card, showing that this relationship has the potential to develop into something more meaningful. Both of these cards together show that the relationship is likely to bring opportunities to grow and find fulfilment for both individuals. The Empress in the position of Challenge shows what may cause problems in the relationship, or at least what will need to be faced in order for the relationship to thrive. On a literal level, the Empress may imply that having children could become an issue for the couple, perhaps with one partner more positive about the idea than the other. On a deeper level, it may suggest that one partner will find themselves "mothering" the other, with that partner putting more emotional energy into the relationship than the other. It could also mean that the couple will become so engrossed in their passion and pleasure in being together, that they neglect their duties or responsibilities. If you are reading for yourself, you will have a sense of which of these layers of meaning is most relevant. If you are reading for someone else, asking them some gentle questions, without prying, can help you both to figure out the energies going on. With a spread like this which flags up a potential challenge, the querent then has some concrete information to take away. In this case, they may decide to get clear on their own feelings about having children before talking to their partner. They may decide to draw some boundaries around how much emotional energy they are investing in "looking after" their partner, or they may realise that they are the one being looked after and resolve to do the same for their partner. The important thing is that they have a sense of how they can use the information the tarot has given them.

# THE CELTIC CROSS

The Celtic Cross is perhaps the most well known of all tarot spreads. It contains ten cards, set out in a cross shape consisting of the first six cards, with the remaining four in a column at the side.

1.    Your current situation

2.    What is challenging or opposing you at present

These two cards together represent the current energies around the querent, summing up the situation. The second card is usually an opposing energy to the first. This doesn't necessarily mean that the first card is positive and the

244

second more challenging. If the querent is currently going through a challenging time, the second card may offer a more positive input.

3.      Conscious mind / higher self

4.      Hidden or unconscious influences

The cards above and below the central cross show the querent's state of mind. The bottom card reflects what is hidden, but may unconsciously be the driver for the current situation. The top card can show what is on the querent's mind, what she is most conscious of at this time. It also gives a sense of the highest potential available.

5.      Past

6.      Immediate future

The two cards to the right and left of the central cross are the timeline so that the central line of the reading is past, present and future. The Future card here shows the immediate future, perhaps if no action is taken or changes are made.

7.      Your inner self

The first card of the outside column shows how the querent is feeling, how they see the situation and also see themselves, and how these affect the situation in question.

8.      External influences

This card reflects the environment or circumstances around the querent, and how these factors might affect the question.


9.    Hopes and fears


This card shows how the querent's attitudes or assumptions might affect the course of events.


10.    Final outcome


The final outcome brings all the other cards together, combining the influences of the whole reading to give a possible or likely outcome. As with any tarot reading, this outcome is not fixed, and if it causes concern to the querent its common to pull one or two more cards to seek clarity on why such an outcome may happen, or how to avoid it.

# A SAMPLE READING USING THE CELTIC CROSS

The reading illustrated, using the Tarot of Marseilles, is for a querent asking what she needs to know about her career at this time. There are only two Major Arcana cards, and neither of them is in the central cross, showing that any changes are likely to feel more like an evolution than a revolution. There are quite a few cards which fall late in the number sequence, such as Tens and Eights, and also two which come at the beginning, an Ace and a Two. This suggests that there may be a phase ending and a new chapter beginning for the querent.


1.      King of Wands

The King of Wands as her current situation shows that she is already well established in her career, confident in her knowledge and able to take the lead both to direct others and to keep her own focus.


2.      Two of Wands

The Two of Wands in the opposing position shows that she may be seeking something new, making the decision to step away from what she has been doing so far and seek a new challenge.

3.  Ten of Cups

The Ten of Cups is a card of emotional abundance, and in the position of Conscious mind / higher self is suggests that she is currently very aware of her emotions and how they are affecting her. It may be that she loves her job, or possibly that she finds it overwhelming in some way. On the other hand, this card could be an indication that what is on her mind is more focused on family and feelings, and she is ready to leave the high flying career behind.

4.  Eight of Cups

As the unconscious influence, the Eight of Cups reinforces the possibility that the querent is ready to move on in some way. When this card appears in a reading, it usually means that the querent is seeking something more meaningful, a move out of their comfort zone towards a more fulfilling path.

5.  Ten of Pentacles

The Ten is the end of the number cycle and generally indicates that we have reached a culmination point. It may suggest that the querent needs to be careful not to focus so much on the material that she neglects her Ten of Cups feelings. In this position, the Ten of Pentacles suggests that she has built up a good level of material security, and now she is ready for a new, perhaps more meaningful challenge.

6.  Ace of Swords

In the Future position, the Ace of Swords brings in a brand new energy and is the only Swords card in the reading. This might suggest that the querent has not focused too much on her intellect in her career so far, but that now she is ready for study or some new ideas.

7.  The Chariot

In the position of Self, the Chariot indicates that the querent knows what she wants, and what she needs to do to get it. It suggests that she is a person with lots of control and focus, who doesn't hold back when she has set her mind to something.


8.     Seven of Cups

In contrast to the Self position, the Seven of Cups as outside influences may suggest that other people see the querent as lacking in focus or following an unrealistic dream. It might also suggest that those around her are making suggestions about what she should do, whereas she already knows, as indicated by the Chariot in the previous position. The Seven of Cups here might also suggest that people keep trying to "tempt" the querent off her intended course by giving her other options.


9.     The Emperor

As her card of hopes and fears, the Emperor may suggest that the querent wants to take a more responsible role in her career, perhaps moving into management or leadership. This is backed up by the King of Wands in the centre position. On the other hand, she may feel blocked by somebody who is already in such a position, or perhaps be fearful of losing control.


10.     Page of Pentacles

The Page of Pentacles is in the position of the final outcome, and like the Ace of Swords in the Future position suggests studying, or at least following a new path. The Pages bring a sense of curiosity and fascination to whatever they do, and this card suggests that taking such an approach is what the querent needs to revitalise her career.

# NEXT STEPS IN YOUR TAROT JOURNEY

As well as doing tarot readings, there are many other ways to use the cards which you can explore as you get to know them. There are many books and online resources giving spreads for just about every question under the sun, and in time you may also want to start inventing your own spreads. Keeping a tarot journal is a very useful exercise. In it, you can note down your daily cards, and keep a record of readings done for yourself and others. Over time your journal can become a valuable resource. You will be able to see the patterns in the cards that appear for you, how their meaning applies to your life and how that may change over time.

A powerful way to work with the cards and build a strong personal connection with them is to meditate on them or use them for visualisation. If you've never done this before, it may take a little practice, but its definitely worth persevering. The easiest way to begin is simply to journey in your imagination into the image on the card. To do this, find a time and place when you won't be disturbed, and somewhere you can sit or lie down comfortably. You may like to light a candle to indicate to your higher self that this is a meaningful process. Take a few minutes to relax your body and your breathing, and then hold the card in front of you and gaze lightly at the image. After a few minutes, close your eyes and hold the image in your mind. Once you have it there clearly, you can step into the image, moving from a two-dimensional version to a three-dimensional version. Using your active imagination, travel around inside the image, perhaps talking to the figures there or simply exploring. When you have finished, step back out of the image and into your body, and note your experiences in your journal.

Getting to know the tarot cards can be the journey of a lifetime, and there will always be something new to learn. As with all the best things in life, the most important thing is to enjoy the journey!